W9-AKV-432

Freeing the Firefly

Discovering an Uncontainable God

by

Mike Christie

1st edition: June 26, 2018

ISBN: 9781732320901

Cover art by Mike Christie

For more writing and projects and all that jazz, visit
mkechristie.net or keep up with my instagram @m.christie

TABLE OF CONTENTS

Each night in June
Many of us
Somewhere
Chase a light that flashes
And then hides
And then flashes

All of us
In our daily rhythm
The same

Our great pursuit and capture
Resulting in no light to remain

Where observation ends
And conquest begins
Recognition dies.

Along with the firefly

Grandpa,

Your recollection of times past with a sense of wonder, your embodiment of love, and your instillment of purpose has led to this. You always said I'd write a book. Here it is.

This, above all else, is for you. Thank you.

- mikey

A Brief Note

Wendell Berry has a poem titled The Country of Marriage that ends with the line, "This poem no more mine than any mans who has ever loved a woman."

Berry is writing about his specific experience. And yet, he acknowledges that his specific experience mirrors the collective experience of all men who sit in his shoes.

Although I'm not anywhere near the writer that Berry is, I'd like to think of this book in a similar light when it comes to the process of reshaping ones faith. You'll find my experience here, but I hope it speaks to yours as well.

This book is one part narrative, one part random tangent, one part fan-girling over bands, all parts ramblings from a millennial. Initially the writing within its bunds were a deeply personal thing. I journaled for days on end at Rockwood Bakery on the South Hill in Spokane. I was processing through life and how my spirituality had shifted over the past five or so years. More and more words spilled out of me. Some formed a story, others were just blurbs or metaphors that I felt embodied some of the ideas of the last five years. But the more I wrote, the more I realized that I might have a book on my hands.

My story isn't all that unique. I haven't gone through any overly difficult trials or tribulations. All I've done is the thing the rest of you have done — live my life. And in living it and being intrigued by the spiritual side of things, I've often thought about what God is, how God is, where God is, etc. I grew up a Christian. But then I got sick of a lot of the faith's tenants. So I walked away from it. And then I rediscovered God in more progressive circles of that faith and others, in poetry, and through my own participation with this world. The works of people like Rob Bell, Mary Oliver, Peter Rollins, and countless others clued me into a more mystical version of God. Mystical meaning not easy to pin down. A bit like the wind or a river or a backyard of fireflies.

This book is simply a personal reflection and recount of that process. If it inspires you or moves you or causes you to think in any way, that's a total bonus. I'm so humbled and grateful you have chosen to put this book in your hands. If you want to converse about any of its ideas or ideas of your own, please, please contact me through my website!

Mike Christie
mikechristie.net

Preface

I was born and raised in Michigan, which meant cars and lakes and recessions and hockey games and snow and—fireflies. Beetle bugs playing the role of little lanterns that litter and linger in the night sky. Swaying and dancing. Appearing and disappearing.

Fireflies were part of my formative years.

I remember nights where I'd chase them around the yard of my house with neighborhood friends. They'd glow for a second, and we'd try to clasp them in our cupped hands before they disappeared back into the dark. When their light would fade, another would appear, and we'd chase after that one, and then it would disappear, and then another one somewhere else. There was a consistent excitement that came with the light, and dreaded anticipation that came with the dark. Then, after much chasing and concentration, we'd finally catch one and put it in a mason jar. We'd add some grass, tighten some saran wrap over the top, and stick our jars by the sides of our beds.

. . .

Early on in the development of my Christian faith, my understanding of God was rooted in a framework a writer named Peter Rollins gave me language for years later. I saw God as a *super being*. As a bigger, better, stronger, and mightier version of Superman. God was something I could clearly contain, and whose identification was man, might, and masculinity.

God was against *that* and for *this*, and each one of those categories had parameters that made sense and were tangible, clear, and defined. God had bounds so that God could be God (supposedly), and evil could be evil (supposedly); and in this light the framework of what God was and what evil was existed in the binaries of peace and comfort for God, and disobedience and sin for evil.

I could carry God close to me because I could contain God. God, a being I had framed as *Him*, was a construct that I could hold onto and feel safe with because of the parameters in which I had placed him. And this construct was very helpful! I didn't ever have to venture into the territory of feeling uncomfortable with a belief I didn't like because I could simply rebuke the belief as not being from God.

But belief that doesn't lead to growth can often become detrimental.

With this God I had, there was no risk, discovery, or mystery. God was God, and what God was and wasn't was marked, clear, and set.

This mentality should sound similar to the way of tradition. Within tradition there is a way things are *supposed to be*. But whatever the *supposed to be* reality within tradition happens to be is rarely the reality allowing room for ideas to evolve, become, and flourish.

. . .

Inevitably, the morning after I had caught that firefly, I would look over to the jar beside my bed and lay my eyes on the dead remains of something that, just the evening before, had been full of life and wonder in the night sky. You can catch a firefly in a jar, and for awhile it will have the same glow it initially had. But solitude and containment cause the light to fade. Or, more objectively speaking, the firefly suffocates and dries out.

This suffocation occurs because all givers and receivers of life need space to grow, and all bearers of light need space to expand.

I think my superman God is dead too. Because as hard as I tried to contain whatever *he* was, I realized that wouldn't, shouldn't and perhaps most importantly, couldn't work. I grew up, and I began to see God where God, according to my closed jar faith, wasn't supposed to be seen.

I witnessed the love of people in same-sex relationships, and that love seemed more real and alive than the relationships of some of the heterosexual couples I knew. I read about other religions and read books by the accused false teachers of my own religion and realized that God was perhaps more active in those places than a lot of the church services I went to. I listened to a lot of music that was not labeled Christian and realized that God's voice was often singing much louder in those songs.

God shifted from superman to river.

From definition to a way of expression.

From category to a theme.

We all need to catch a firefly in a mason jar and witness that firefly die in order to realize how much more beautiful it is for the firefly to exist with space to be and fly and dance with the rest of its kind. We all need to have a contained and rule-based God in order to see just how much that belief doesn't work as we enter into and see the true reality and way of this world beyond our limited context.

Instead of trying to catch or categorize God, I began to simply let God be. And when I did that, I began to see this Divine and beautiful Insistence dance around me freely. Containment didn't work anymore. It didn't have to work anymore.

I was home one summer during college when this new reality or framework made its presence known through a fitting and familiar image. My family had recently moved into a new house over Christmas break the year before. The house sits on top of a ridge, and at the bottom of the ridge, there is a grove with an abundance of oak and maple trees that line the hillside. Toward the bottom of the ravine, there is a creek with lush, tall grasses. The leaves are so thick above you that the sky is greener than it is blue during the day. It's quite the surreal setting.

It was late June, and I was sitting out on the back patio with my guitar, strumming some basic chords, when it began to happen—the fireflies came out.

First one. And then two. Three. Seven. Twelve. Twenty.

Until there were so many that you couldn't count them anymore; not necessarily because of their quantity but because when one firefly illuminated, another one went dark, and another illuminated, and another went dark. And so on.

When it's dark outside, you can't count the number of fireflies there are. Unless, of course, you only experience one at a time because you are trying to catch them. When you focus on the collective group of these lantern-butted bugs, the night sky becomes a blank canvas where you can see one appear in one place. Then disappear. And then another one appears in another place, and then disappears. The number is not tangible or quantifiable or definable or even relevant. It's simply light existing freely and fluidly.

The fireflies shine their light anywhere and everywhere at the same time, seemingly with no set path or direction. But when they illuminate, you know without question what it is you are witnessing. Fireflies outside the mason jar cast light in any place you can imagine. And you don't question why or how. You just lose your breath in the wonder of it all.

What I have begun to understand simply by realizing just how little of this world I comprehend is that God, when released from our grasp, exists everywhere. And you don't have to question why or how or what, you simply just know. Labeling the residence of the Divine isn't sustainable. It doesn't work with something that is much more thematic than specific.

God is not superman, but superseding. Superseding any category or confines or captivity we house *him* in. God is not gender. God is event. And event can happen in any space, at any time, and in any context. My personal experience has led me to believe that the Insistence of the Divine or God or Spirit or Way or whatever you want to call it, can happen much more freely when we put down the mason jar and instead choose to look upon the canvas of our lives, and see the light swirling all around us.

Once you give yourself over to the way of the wild nature of the light, you don't question what the light is. You just know. And then you see the light appear in another place.

And another.

And another.

And before you know it, it's all around you.

The Boxes We Live In

One of my favorite podcasts is called *On Being*. It features the NPR talk show host Krista Tippett, and describes itself as a program focusing on, "the big questions of meaning." Tippett interviews all sorts of people. From theoretical physicists to poets, from experts on brain chemistry to spiritual sages. The gamut for Tippett's guests is a wide one. Which is fitting. Because, in my experience, that's how the way of meaning seems to operate.

One guest Tippett had on was a guy by the name of Richard Rohr. Rohr is one of the few people Tippett has chatted with that I had heard of prior to listening to the interview. I listened to the interview the summer after I graduated from college. I had the privilege of meeting Rohr when I was a college sophomore at a conference I attended. I was a big fan of his work. But even for how good Rohr's writing tends to be, it's his ability to effectively communicate abstract ideas that baffles me time and time again. So, when I saw he was featured on my favorite podcast, I put the interview on the next time I got in my car.

In the interview, Tippett does a great job getting Rohr to touch on the wide-ranging topics he's so literate in. He's specialized in mysticism, psychological development, and Christian theology as a whole. Early on in the conversation, Rohr brought up something concerning human spiritual development and the course spiritual development must take.

According to Rohr, there are three main boxes everyone must work through in life.

Box number one is order. This box is characterized by orthodoxy, tradition, rules, and dualistic thinking. By thought that is black and white. Sacred versus secular. Heaven or hell. Good or evil. Rohr says that just as we learn to think this way cognitively early on, most spiritual dynamics spend all their time here. Focusing on taking in what is *good* and keeping out what is *bad*.

Box number two is disorder. Rohr says this is where liberal and progressive thought can get stuck. It's the place of the university. Subversion and rethinking are what this box is made up of. Authority and tradition fall by the wayside to make way for individualism and personal identity shaping.

Box number three is reorder. This box is a place that takes the order one has found in life, reshapes it, breaks it down through the process of disorder, and then creates something new and fresh. This third box isn't afraid of paradox, but also isn't seeking to disrupt any and every notion for the sake of disruption. It isn't characterized by *this or that* but by *both and*. Box number three sees the world, not as a series of rights and wrongs, or a place of chaos, but as a place of order amidst the chaos.

Upon listening to this interview, I realized how abundantly true this notion of order, disorder, and reorder is. And how this notion exists everywhere and through every experience. And how you are never really done going through the process of these three boxes, but instead are encountering the boxes over and over. Your mind may take a particular lens of seeing the world that lines up with one of these three ways of perception more often than others, but when you become conscious of these perceptions, you see how prevalent they are in every aspect of your life.

. . .

My life, just like yours, has been made up of an initial phase of order, a phase of disorder, and then eventual reorder. And this book is a bit of my story, based on this three-part series. This book is a bit of a commentary on how even if order can be nice and safe, and disorder can be subversive and fun, reorder seems to be the place where we see the world most purely.

And the way we come to this place is through progress.

We must venture through the cycle. Keep walking. Keep pushing forward.

I see order as the firefly in the jar. Disorder as that firefly dying from suffocation. And reorder as the fireflies all around, with no intent to catch them. This book is a bit of my story intertwined with a few random thoughts and essays as to how that cycle has played out for me. I hope it clues you into how much this process is happening in your life too.

Progress

People progress. It's what we do. Both literally and figuratively. No matter where you are now, at this moment, reading this book, you have gotten here from some other place. This idea of progress is true in both a literal way and a metaphorical sense. We humans move.

This movement is why we are still alive today. Hundreds of thousands of years ago, the earth had a species very similar to us known as the Neanderthal. Those Neanderthals are thought to have been smarter than us Homo sapiens. More capable. More conscious. But there was one thing us Homo sapiens were more prone to than they —we moved. This is why we refer to people who are lazy as Neanderthals. Because Neanderthals were content to lounge around and stay put.

Homo sapiens chose to venture into the great unknown. They spread out from Ethiopia to the edges of the earth.

People like the Polynesians set out into the Pacific in wooden boats and eventually created societies on the islands of Hawaii and Tahiti, thousands of miles from the spot of their origin.

Native Americans walked from the tip of the northern hemisphere all the way down to the tip of the southern and settled in pockets along the way.

We send people into the depths of the ocean, into complete darkness, and into an ecosystem totally unfit for us because we want to explore.

We send people into outer space. Think about that. Into the cosmos. For what end?

Exploration. Movement. Progress.

Movement is literally in our DNA. And it is movement that has kept us alive. Allowed us to progress. It's all because we acted on potential.

And just as we move and explore and venture into the unknown physically, part of the uniqueness of human life is the ability to progress in thought, too. To move past notions we once had and to open ourselves up to new understandings. To be part of the story. To move from catching fireflies to seeing them.

Neuroscientists now know that throughout our whole life our brains never stop developing. They are always growing and evolving. We as human beings are never done learning and expanding.

And that is why story is so important. Story is imperative because it is the canvas on which this growth paints itself. It is through story that we witness a movement. A trajectory. The purpose revealed through theme. I currently teach English to high schoolers, and one of the things I talk about with them is that there are two ways you can read a book. You can read to find out what *happens*, or you can read to see what is *happening*. The distinction is key. Focusing on what happens makes you miss the intricacies of every page you pass over. You miss the journey toward revelation when you focus on the end.

It is in our steps that we discover. Slowly but steadily.

I grew up in a religious system where a lot of people believed because of what they could attain—eternal life. That is the Christianity I learned about in church. Faith was not a framework, but a means to an end. And I've talked to countless people who believe the same thing. They're trying to catch something. Salvation. Just like I tried to catch those fireflies.

But I had a shift. It started gradually, over time, and hasn't stopped happening. It was a shift to see the world in a step-by-step kind of way. A way of progress that was full of the sacred in every moment. A moment of living into eternity now. Instead of focusing on what was to happen, I began trying to focus on what was happening. Every day. In every breath. With every new phase.

This reordering was not easy. It took time. And I still am unable to do this with every moment of every day, obviously. But what I've discovered is that watching the story unfold clues you in to a lot of the nuances and beauty of the story, much more than knowing a possible ending to the story does.

This way of being is modeled in so many wonderful, wise people throughout history, spanning the gamut of multiple religions. But what surprised me more than anything was the reality that this truth seemed to be something that my faiths figurehead, Jesus, has spoken to all along. Jesus wasn't ever focused on getting me or anyone somewhere else. He was focused on getting me and us to recognize the kingdom, the beauty, the potential, right now. Here In this world. In every step.

Moving In

When you grow up in a nondenominational church for most of your life, you don't really understand the minefield-clad scope of theology. But when you grow up in such nondenominational circles because your family quickly uprooted from the Catholic masses you were accustomed to, you begin to think there is a reality of animosity in religious systems. This was my reality. And I felt a bit caught between the two.

I grew up Catholic. And that Catholicism was primarily a way of tradition prescribed to my parents, who then prescribed it to my siblings and I. But I also grew up with a mother who didn't take too kindly to bogus acts of corruption. And when she saw this going on in the Catholic church we were a part of, we left.

In fourth grade, a jump from incense and white robes landed me, along with the rest of my family, in a world of fancy lighting and fog machines.

Our new church home was Christianity made big. It was faith that filled up stadiums. And it did those things with loud music and a theology of *dos* and *don'ts*, simplifying the historical traditions most people in its cushioned seats were fleeing from. Our family included.

I had been too young at this time to understand the theology we were leaving. Theology was formed here in this hyper-produced, megachurch culture for me. And all I understood it as was redundant youth group sermons. Sermons that talked about how you shouldn't do drugs or drink or have sex before marriage. I understood God to be a prescriber of don'ts. Not a spectrum of Calvinism versus Arminianism[1]. Or unconditional election versus free will. Or substitutionary atonement versus original blessing. Theology was simply a binary option of two paths to walk - one of life and Jesus. And one of death and Satan.

The irony is that whether you are sick of the narrow-minded views of conservative and highly academic churches or are sick of the monotonous youth groups of user-friendly churches with thousands in attendance each weekend, I've found from talking with many people that the angst you feel can take you to the same place—the books of Rob Bell.

By the summer after my senior year of high school, I was in the perfect place to be received with open arms into the current of progressive thought. That season of obscene Michigan humidity was full of hesitant and self-conscious

---

[1] These two terms, Calvinism / Arminianism, are two differing perspectives on theology. An oversimplified definition is that calvinist believe in predeterminism, arminians believe in free will.

angst. Hooking up with girls, one of which was dating my best friend, smoking weed for the first time, drinking too much alcohol, and sneaking into the local ice rink past midnight to drink beer and play hockey with buddies.

I was the nightmare every youth group leader wakes up from.

. . .

In downtown Royal Oak, the suburb of Detroit I grew up in, there is a building. A building that was once a place of imagination, loitering, coffee dates, plenty of CDs, and— heresy. This building, now a Buffalo Wild Wings, was a Barnes & Noble.

Upon hearing me reminisce about the night before, where I had participated in some of the aforementioned rebellion, my mom had her suspicions confirmed that her once easy-to-raise son was experiencing a bit of post-high school identity shifting. And her mind came up with an idea involving said magical building. As we ate quesadillas in the cafeteria of the Detroit Institute of Arts she, as the sage she was, is, and always will be, didn't ridicule or demean, but suggested something.

"I don't support those decisions, but you're an adult now. You can do what you do. But before you leave for school, could you do me a favor? What if on the way back home, we stop by Barnes & Noble? You pick out a book for us to read together over the rest of the summer. We can find time once a week to discuss it over brunch."

I liked eggs, and I also liked books, and I loved the smell of Barnes & Noble, so we stopped on our way back from the museum

I scoured bookshelves looking for something I could use my recently acquired skills of postmodern deconstruction from my AP Literature class on. But then I caught a glimpse of a book with a cover full of cool red and blue triangles.

The paragraphs inside were full of bold words and line breaks.

The book's name, *What We Talk About When We Talk About God*, lured in a kid who, when at youth group, would try to talk about God, only to be told that's not what we talk about when we talk about God…

I was sold.

It's important to note that although this particular season was one of liberating angst, I had always been profoundly curious about spirituality, even if not well versed in the more academic realms of theology. This curiosity was largely due to a wonderful small group I had in high school. The group was led by a guy named Charlie, but it only lasted for my first three years of high school. Charlie walked away from it my senior year because he didn't really know what he believed anymore. Which, quite frankly, had been the general vibe for the majority of the time our group was together. And, as these things work, was probably what made it so great. However, during my senior year, I was the only remaining by-product of the group. And the questions I asked during the new group I was placed in, although questions Charlie would have likely loved, were met with hostility by others.

What I didn't know then, but know now, is that I was a budding mystic. And questions stemming from this frame of mind are largely not within the frame of mind of carefully-packaged youth groups at megachurches. This led to the summer reading of *What We Talk About When We Talk About God* being a much needed, refreshing, and long-deep breath of fresh air for me.

My mom and I were both loving it. It led us to start talking about and thinking about words like *ruach* which means breath and wind and spirit in Hebrew, and how amazing the implications of that were.

And how God moves in ticks. From point a to point b. Point b to point c. That God ultimately is pushing society forward, not pulling us back.

And how freeing it was not to be bound by a religion based on what *not* to do. But instead, to open yourself up to a spirituality cluing you in on what you have the possibility to see when you seek out and allow mystical encounters with Christ to happen. Mystical not in a floaty / magic type of way. But in a way that is open to seeing God through the trees, the birds, the taste of a meal, etc.

I was enamored. And, weeks before I went to college, I had a whole new pulse tied to the life of my spiritual self.

But a bit about college.

When I was in fifth grade, I would come home from school and sit in front of my computer. Not to play games but to spend hours upon hours exploring the world on Google Earth. I learned about Pacific atolls with lagoons full of sharks, searched for aliens amidst Area 51, and discovered and developed a love for the lake I would later propose to my wife on the shores of some eleven or so years later.

My greatest discovery of all, however, was a little slice in the upper left corner of our country known as the Pacific Northwest. As an eleven-year-old, I was enraptured by the place. Looking at it from a satellite perspective drew out the same curiosity in me that looking at the map of Narnia C.S Lewis included before his tales beyond the wardrobe garnered just a couple years prior.

So, as you do as an eleven-year-old, I told my parents I'd live there one day, in the Pacific Northwest.

And so, as you do as an eighteen-year-old, I found a school out there to attend.

But because any school in the Northwest would be an out-of-state school, the school had to be affordable. And because I was into spirituality and religion and philosophy, it had to have programs in those areas. And because I wanted only to have to take six roads to get back to my home in Michigan, even if I was 2,000 miles away, it had to be off I-90...

And wouldn't you know it, little old Mike discovered the *very* little, and often overlooked, Spokane campus of one of the most conservative Christian schools in all of America—

Moody Bible Institute.

So, let's review,

1. I was born and raised in the Catholic church. And, even if my family made the switch in fifth grade to nondenominational, megachurch land, I had never been baptized out of the Catholic church (I, like you, may not have seen any problem with this. But you, like I wasn't, likely aren't aware of the priorities of a conservative Christian school).

2. I had recently taken a liking to drinking, partying, hooking up with multiple girls, hooking up with my best friend's girl, and a little green plant. Moody didn't allow students to dance, let alone drink, smoke, or allow man and woman to be alone together in the same room for any reason.

3. My theology was a combination of Derrida-inspired deconstructionism and Bell's twenty-first century Christian mysticism. And I had committed myself to a school where John Calvin, the father of predestination, might as well be president.

My mom and I were halfway through *What We Talk About When We Talk About God* when I joined the Facebook group for the incoming class at Moody. Upon seeing all of the posts people were making about the books they were reading that summer, I was moved to talk about the book sitting in my lap. As I began to type out how much I loved the new Rob Bell book, my mom earnestly stopped me before hitting the post button.

"Why don't you just wait on that one and talk to people about it in person," she said.

Confused, but finding undying respect for my mother's opinion during that stage because of our little book club, I obliged.

My understanding of the spectrum of theology was NONE. I knew that people at youth group didn't like Bell, but I thought that was a result of his book called *Sex God* and my youth group hated the idea of sex outside the context of males and females and marriage. I didn't know who Calvin was, other than a place I considered going to school to play golf at, and the only Martin Luther I really cared about was a King.

As the summer came to a close, five of the six of us Christies piled into a minivan and made the five-day trek from Michigan to Washington. We stopped in the Badlands, Glacier National Park, and saw things a midwesterner cannot even produce in the context of his or her dreams. Mountains and lakes and forests of crippling beauty.

We arrived at the Moody house I would spend the next year living in with seven other Moody men. The first priority in room setup was, of course, working with my little brother, Colin, to install a speaker system I got at my graduation party, in addition to the subwoofer that came with it. Klipsch's finest. Said speaker, upon completion of installation, blared "I Am a God" by Kanye West in a house full of guys who had something ingrained in them as foreign to me as this new landscape known as *conservative theology.*

Next in the room setup came my books, of which there was now another Bell work in the collection, *Jesus Wants to Save Christians* (not Jesus Wants to Save the Elect, much to the dismay of my peers, unbeknownst to me).

Happy-go-lucky Mike was grinning ear to ear. He was in the Northwest! Ponderosa pines and mountains galore! Meanwhile, the other seven guys were checking their acceptance emails making sure they were in the right place.

My family and I went to PF Chang's in downtown Spokane. We were emotionally spent and knew it would only get worse with my family's looming departure. I looked around the table at my Dad, a man of consistent dependability and love. My Mom, a true kindred spirit, and equal part friend and parent. Catherine, a younger sister with many arguments in our past, but a kindness so tangible. And Colin, the cool dude, my younger brother who was, is, and always will be my best friend. My older brother Jack was back home in Michigan in school. The goodbye to him, the one who inspired me to take a chance and move in the first place, was also fresh in my mind.

It was such an emotionally vulnerable place. And my mind had a hard time taking it all in.

We left the restaurant and decided it would be best for me to spend the night in the house with the guys. My family would pick me up the next morning for a final breakfast before they left. I came back inside the sea-foam green home, built in 1907, and found everyone conversing in the kitchen. I joined and was greeted with the first theological question of my first year of theological education:

"What do you think of Rob Bell," asked a fellow housemate, with a certain leading candor in his voice, to our RA.

My RA responded, "I don't necessarily think he's going to hell himself, but I think he's leading a lot of people there."

And thus began my freshman year of college.

The Fight or Flight Nature within a Religion of Love

Moody was full of opportunities to learn just how much people within the same realm of thought could attack each other over nuance.

This, my friends, is the epitome of religion.

What I encountered was a spectrum swinging from one extreme of Arminianism (again, think free will) to the other, Calvinism (again, think predeterminism). The difficult thing about such a spectrum is that even within it, there are agreed-upon norms that you don't go against.

I basically went against all of them.

When it was considered a liberal perspective to believe that hell was annihilation rather than eternal conscious torment at Moody, I was busy questioning if hell was really even a place of postmortem existence or just a state of mind. A state of mind I, ironically, seemed to be finding myself in a lot at this school debating such topics.

A liberal belief at Moody was believing the earth was over 10,000 years old but still literally created by God. The dominant belief at Moody was that it was younger than 10,000 years old, and literally created by God. I, meanwhile, was reading up on Darwin and the big bang theory. Becoming entranced by the poetic nature of evolution when seen through the lens of human progress and developing consciousness. A thread of thought my peers saw as a compromise on the authority of God's word.

I distinctly remember sitting in a writing 101 class in which I built a thesis around the idea that all religions, in their purest sense, were different wells accessing the same underground river. This is an idea based off of a Buddhist philosophy I fell in love with early on during this shift of perspective. A fellow student in the class, while reading my paper, let out little giggles every thirty seconds or so.

This laughter was rather discouraging. Grammar had always been a weakness of mine, but this much laughter had to mean there were some serious, and consistent, lapses in my writing. But when my classmate was done reading, the first thing he did was grin and tell me how great I was at writing satire through the lens of liberal theology.

He thought my whole paper was a satire. Because if you went to Moody, you definitely didn't believe what I was writing.

There was another instance where I asked to do a book

report on a highly controversial book by the author that (get ready for irony) inspired me to go to this school. This book was what caused Bell to be labeled as a heretic by many. It is called *Love Wins*, and it questions the views of hell that many in evangelical Christianity held, and continue to hold. The professor, known for his wit and happy-go-lucky demeanor, immediately became placid.

He wanted to make sure my stance would be one that was critical. Because Bell had "gone off the deep end," he told me. I was caught in an awkward spot of wanting to pester him as to why he thought this way. But the idea of picking your battles settled into my mind. And after his tangent about Bell's dangerous theology was over, I replied simply,

"I'm sure I'll find some things to be critical about after reading it."

I turned in the paper never to receive it back at the end of the semester. I followed up the following semester with attempts to track it down. The professor never got back to me, and I received a very poor grade on it.

I met a few buddies who were integral to my sanity during this time—Grant, Phil, Colt, and Harold. And although to most of them my theology was coined with the term—a slippery slope, a phrase of passive aggressive disagreement —we could at least entertain ideas with each other over donuts and carafes of coffee at the local staple, Donut Parade.

We talked about Rollins' parables and atheism as the truest form of theism, due to its lack of putting a bound on who or what God was. We talked about pantheism, mostly due to their questions directed at Phil and me as to whether or not we were pantheists, largely because of our love for tree metaphors. We'd get academic and talk about how it was not pantheism we identified with, but panentheism, which is the idea that God isn't all, but superseding through all. This is different from the pantheist belief that God is literally all things. Both of which were heretical in the minds of superiors I talked to about such things at Moody.

And then we'd take another bite of donut and another sip of coffee.

There was a general curiosity in this group of friends. A type of curiosity we each felt likely wasn't welcomed in our classrooms. Which yielded a great lesson which many have spoken to: learning is the act of being curious. And finding places where curiosity can flourish is essential. And so we did just that. We took camping trips together, drank more coffee, and went on walks. It was a group of friends essential to my time at Moody. People without people are merely blobs attempting to find purpose but not making any progress.

Donut Parade shut down, as did those friendships. Except for Phil appearing at my wedding a few years later.

It is things with a shelf life that give us the nourishment to make it through one phase of life with enough fuel to push onto the next. These guys were that.

Dealing with Shelf Life

Moody was a complicated time for my ability to process, though. I knew I wouldn't be there more than a year. I had every intention of leaving after one year because of how much I felt outside the dominant consciousness of the place. There were positives. I had good friends like the ones mentioned previously. I also had a mentor from a church outside of Moody named Jason, and his family was my family away from family. And there was my housemate dynamic, which, apart from the occasional debates about homosexuality or hell or whether Jesus hit people with the whips he had in the marketplace or just drove them out by lashing near them, was full of laughter and memories.

And there were camping trips and inner tubing down snowy mountains and pranks.

But there was also the reality of confronting the fact that I was not seen as having valid or justifiable opinions by most of my peers, and definitely not by my professors. And as much as the angsty spirit in me from the previous summer found satisfaction in pushing against the grain, it was also profoundly lonely in a spiritual sense. Who I am as a person is, well, emotional. I process the world through how I feel. That coupled with a need to be authentic (yes, I am a *four* for those familiar with the Enneagram) left me in a place of uncertainty and, quite frankly, a pain of the soul.

A Turning Point

Moody had something a couple of times a month called Athanasius lectures for their honors students. For those of you that aren't familiar, Athanasius was a bishop during the fourth century who was known as "the one standing over the defeated heretic." Seeing as I had been called, or my theology, more accurately, had been called, *heretical* fairly frequently during this period of my life, these were wonderfully welcoming events for people like me—

Yeah, not really.

But the students who spoke at these lectures always brought cookies as bribes to get other students to show up. And if there is a cookie in attendance, there is a bound to be a Mike there as well.

There was one particular lecture that my buddy Jake, who was my roommate and later one of my groomsmen, and I went to. The lecture's topic for analysis was five-point

Calvinism and the legitimacy of it. Not even just the legitimacy, but the necessity in holding this belief for sound theology.

Jake is highly objective and stoic. I am highly subjective and emotional. Jake sees academics as an interesting thing to taste in his mouth. I swallow everything, and have either a warm stomach or have to puke. That being said, we both encountered this lecture very differently.

It was a turning point for me.

The student speaking outlined how the premise of TULIP, the acronym at the basis of five-point Calvinism, was the only way one could interpret the theology of Paul, the author of many books in the New Testament, and therefore, theology in general. Here's what the TULIP acronym is, according to yours truly:

Total depravity: Interpreted as you're shit by yourself.

Unconditional Election: God picks favorites. God's elect are the chosen ones, and you have no say in if you are or aren't one of the chosen.

Limited Atonement: If you aren't one of God's favorites, have fun in hell, because not everyone is "covered by the blood of Christ."

Irresistible Grace: Like chocolate espresso cookies, the grace of God, if you are one of the elect, is irresistible. But only if the cookies are baked for you. If not, have fun in the oven with burnt cookies down in hell.

Perseverance of the Saints: Once you are saved, you are always saved. And because it's all predetermined, you're already saved. Unless you're not saved. Then hell. Bye.

Jake sat rubbing his chin; I sat with my jaw on the floor as this student, who was incredibly well read in the Bible and systematic theology, laid out this systematic reasoning as to why this had to be the way things were. He pointed at passages in Romans, one of those New Testament books written by Paul (which I still have trouble reading because of how often it was quoted to me at Moody) and, upon his completion, received raving reviews from professors in attendance. Everyone applauded. People seemed ecstatic. It was as if someone had just, in such a natural and clear fashion, backed up and legitimized the frame for the worldview nearly everyone in attendance held.

I, meanwhile, looked down at the old, gray-green floor. Splotches and dust occupied it. The floor mirrored my mind, which was currently being infiltrated with doubt regarding all the theology I had been reading as a counterargument to my education. The theology that brought me back to faith. The thing that gave me a pulse again. All of it was crumbling.

Everyone in the room was standing over me, and I felt defeated. Athanasius, as I understood him, would've been proud.

Jake had taken his hand away from his chin and was now talking with his arms. Ranting about how amazing and informative the whole talk had been. I needed Jake's objectivity in my life, immensely at times, but now was not one of those moments.

I mumbled something to the effect of "I'll see you back at the house," walked straight past the cookies, and glared directly ahead the whole walk home. When I got back, I went to my room, closed the door, fell flat on my face, and wept.

With tears pooling onto my pillow, I realized I had three options —

1. Adopt this five-point deal. It seemed that according to this kid who spoke tonight, and to the only place I had encountered academic theology, it was the only legitimate Christian option.

2. Become an atheist. Revolt against this vile thing I had just tasted through my experience tonight and bark at how evil religion is to the human psyche.

3. Puke out what I had just tasted, fearlessly push back, and present a new way of thought. The way of thought that I had learned from and gained so much life from that was presented in the books of Bell and others. Give those ideas a Mike Christie twist. And present them in the hive mind-setting I was in as a pushback to their narrow-scoped theology.

And I, as the young budding mystic I was becoming, chose the third way.

Hallelujah for the First Time

In mid-May of that year, I was sitting in Starbucks writing my final paper as a Moody student. I was talking about "this new thing in the air." And quoting Phyllis Tickle on how Christianity was going through a new reformation. And how the push of that reformation was not taking us to a place of biblical literalism like the one 500 years previously yeilded, but to a place of personal encounters through interaction with the Divine.

I quoted Rollins, Rohr, Brian McLaren, Rachel Held Evans, the old favorite Rob Bell, and many others in a bold attempt to put into words all the frustrations I had toward what my education that year had strategically chosen to leave out. Which were all the new places Christianity was headed that I read up on independently.

Ideas that were happening right in front of us during this time period while this education coalesced around people and thinkers from hundreds of years previous living in a different context. It was an empowered paper. Towards the end, I put in the following John Muir quote that has been a bit of a personal mission statement since,

"It's a blessed thing to go free in the light of this world, to see God playing upon everything, as a man would play upon his instrument. His fingers on the lightning and the torrent, on every wave of sea and sky, and every living thing, making altogether sing and shine in sweet accord, the one-love harmony of the universe."

It was a bold move. One that brought me back to the first paper I had written for this professor, the one with the many wells to the same underground river idea. But this time it was with fervor and purpose. There was no way it could be confused as satire this go around. This was serious. It was my closing argument; my document nailed to the door of the place of my education.

Everyone has a Ninety-Five Theses they have to nail somewhere at some point. In one sense to make others aware, but more than anything, to make yourself aware, publicly, of who you've evolved to become. What you now see that you can never unsee. To give life and boldness to a shift in perspective.

And as I typed and listened to a random Spotify radio station, my mind became in tune with the lyrics that followed my fingers across the last few sentences I wrote. And as I listened carefully to the words coming through my headphones, I couldn't help but take the words and use them for one final sentence as my closing remarks.

The chorus from The Head and the Heart song that I heard for the first time at that moment at the Starbucks on Hamilton Ave encapsulated how I felt about owning the fact that I was officially a progressive. Owning the fact that the ways of election and limited atonement and total depravity were things I didn't buy. Owning the fact that I truly felt I was following the voice of the Divine. And chasing after it. And my time at Moody came to a close with the following words from the song "Sounds Like Hallelujah,"

I'm not walking away
I'm just hearing what you're saying.
And for the first time
Sounds like hallelujah for the first time.
For the first time
Singing hallelujah for the first time.

Rethink. Retain. Reimagine.

During the year I was at Moody, I began to do something every millennial believing they hold something of value in their little mind does.

I blogged.

What first began as a place to post papers on the importance of Christianity and ecology becoming more closely acquainted... Or a place for my parents to keep tabs on my academia... Or a place for me to have everything located and accessible for when I'd go home and my grandpa wanted to hear my writing... Or all of those things... Ultimately became an outlet to process, openly to the world, some of the thoughts and frustrations I was having. Life at Moody was a life full of dissonance. Classes were full of historical conservative theology, which I countered by reading endless amounts of counterarguments to when I got back to my house.

Something interesting happens when you are naive enough to think your opinion matters.

Your opinion starts to matter.

And not from the newfound self-importance and ignorant arrogance blogging can at times garner, but more because giving words to thoughts allows you to see firsthand the dissonance you are working through. And a dissonant mind, through a process of purification, can become settled. And perhaps even become a bit of a blessing.

Blogging allowed me to not limit learning to something being consumed, but to relay what was being learned into Mike language. To give my spin on all I was being made aware of. It helped my ideas to develop independently and become clothed in their own character.

When I would hear arguments in class about the Bible being *literal*—even the creation account—I would counter through interaction with the biblical text that saw it as being *literary*. The truth that the best novels point to isn't always literally true, but it is their literary power that transforms the novels into beautiful impressions on the heart. The move from seeing something as *literally* true to seeing its *literary* truth ended up making the Bible and the themes it spoke to even more true to me.

It made the Bible alive and vital, simply by making the importance of the Bible not on the literal vitality of all of its characters. Paradoxical as that may sound, that was my experience.

They say that the best way to understand something is to imitate and then innovate. I was imitating what I had read the likes of Bell say in his blog series at the time, now book, What is the Bible, and then innovating it through the reality of my personal experience. And in a blog post I wrote back then, I spoke to this battle for understanding I was going through:

Have you ever read a book? I'm assuming (or hoping) that you have. While reading that book, was everything revealed to you in the first chapter? Or if this was a series, was everything revealed to you in the first book? Probably not, if so, it was probably a rather lackluster piece of literature and didn't hang around for over 2,000 years. Stories evolve with the progression of time. The same is true with the Bible. The Bible is a story about civilization and God speaking to civilization where they are currently at. To paraphrase Bell, it is a story based on the evolving consciousness of those who the story is being told about.

Over my four years of high school, I took multiple AP English courses. I was introduced to a wide variety of ways and theories on how to interpret literature and also multiple pieces of literature to make what I learned applicable. The main concept that I took away from my studies, and probably the most important concept, is that stories are a work that is reliant on the whole but are also continually headed somewhere. Within the whole of a story, multiple different themes, motifs, and ideas unfold depending on where the reader currently is at in the book. Every story, or at least the ones worth mentioning, have a moment that everything previous becomes resolved and there seems to be some sort of peace within the tale.

I believe the same is true with the Bible, and I believe the resolution we find in it is Jesus. This doesn't mean that everything else told previously in the Old Testament wasn't God, it means that God has moved past the moments that seemed to be full of despair and resolved them with not just the death and resurrection of His son (obviously a largely important part) but also with the teachings of His Son. God's story, or as Bell puts it, Gods "evolving narrative" has a beautiful and transforming resolve with Jesus. Obviously, we are not perfect, and the world is not perfect, but with Jesus, we see the potential and the image of perfection. The image of perfection is not war, or the warped treatment of women, or other concepts that are found in the Old Testament that are seen as coming from God. Those images are reflections of the culture those people were in. The perfection or glory of God is seen in the beauty of how He transforms those ideas into something else. A push forward in a sense, all leading to the character and teachings of Jesus.

These were steps. And you don't get anywhere without those.

Finding My Religion. Sorry R.E.M.

I was beginning to discover my religion, and in ways I hadn't up until this point. And as often as I may have been insecure about feeling like I was simply regurgitating what I was reading from Bell, I began to see the reality of change personally. And it happened by training my eyes to look for new things. To look at my religion with the hope of seeing it unassumingly, without any prior training and just simply witnessing it. And in doing this, I realized that the truth I tasted and encountered most frequently was thematic rather than categorical.

I had to leave the Bible for awhile to see this. I didn't do morning ritualistic devotionals like my housemates at Moody. And that was definitely criticized from time to time by them. But I didn't want to read the Bible through the filter of Moody or Bell; I wanted to leave the Bible as I developed my own filter so I could truly experience it as Mike Christie.

Just recently I was talking with my Mom. She had just gone to see a foot masseuse who had a far loftier title for his practice. It was in the vein of alternative medicine. Such foot massages were supposed to be a remedy for relieving headaches, and my mother said this one did. But she also mentioned the biggest takeaway was the conversation she had with the masseuse.

He was born in the Middle East and as a young boy moved to Italy. When he got there, he went to a Catholic priest and said he wanted to leave the Islamic tradition he was raised in and become Catholic. The priest, who was well aware of the cultural stigma in the west toward Islam and was likely, seeing as he was a priest, partial to Christianity, said he wouldn't lead the boy to conversion until he read the Qur'an objectively. He didn't want him simply leaving a faith because of the filter his new setting placed on it.

This boy, now the man massaging my mother's feet, said that after reading his tradition's sacred text, he had a newfound respect for Islam. He saw pieces in the Qur'an that were beautiful. He still was compelled to Christianity because of the centrality of Christ. But not for reasons engrained in him by his setting or context. The priest walked with the boy through an orientation to Christianity, but made sure that Christ was encountered not as a social safety net, but a reality in, around, apart of, and in union with all things. Christ was not to be seen as something that adopts, but rather something that allows you to see the world in a new, harmonious, interconnected way. And that included the Islam of his upbringing.

Faith, when it is tied to a given social or even theological filter of understanding, is largely divisive and petty and stale. It is through interaction with the world that we live in that can help us understand that faith is served better as a river which partners and carries us on our journey of life rather than a pond we always retreat to for safety.

Which ties back to that Buddhist parable I quoted in my paper at Moody about all religions are wells dipping into the same underground river... No one well is tainted in its natural state; we taint the wells ourselves by seeing one as better than the other. This is true of religion and true of differing theologies within a religion. The one truth that I think will tie us together is the subversive nature of sacrificial and selfless love. Love without expectation or explanation. Love that is free flowing like the river that compels it. The river that's flowing beyond the well of ideology.

Seven Ponds

When I was younger, my grandparents lived on one of seven ponds located about an hour north of where I lived in Michigan. The house sat on top of a slight hill that rose from the water behind the house. In the front, there was a big plot of grass bordered on both sides by a forest that stretched out the the borders of the ten acres that they owned. The forest was made of the deciduous trees Michigan is known for. Maples and oaks and elms swayed when it was windy and prominently stood as a gate between the known and the unknown on the edge of their property.

Off to the side of the house, nearer to the water than woods, there was a barn with an antique blue Ford tracker. Whenever you went into the barn, you were met by the smell of oil, moist firewood, and mothballs. All of which had been lingering in the air for at least the last fifty years I'd assume.

It was a historic place. Not on a grand scale. Simply a history of lineage.

It was also here that I learned of history beyond the realm of that of just my family. My Papa had dug a hole for some reason on the side of the house and outlined the different eras of each layer of rock. On top of that, there was the discovery of arrowheads in the fields out front from Native Americans who once roamed the land freely.

But other discovered rocks took me far into the deep past again as I found stones in the gravel driveway with spiral fossil formations. The likely imprint of ammonites, a now extinct mollusk that called this place, one that used to be all water and is now land, home. They were still imprinted clearly on the rock, even if their last breath happened an estimated sixty-five million years ago. There was a course of history seated between the barn and the driveway spanning a spectrum of millions of years. The history of my family, to the history of ancient mollusks.

Beyond the barn and along the driveway with million-year-old frozen lives littered amongst it, there was a garage hosting a classic car. A Chevy I believe. The garage was a place of avoidance, however. Rumors of a snake who decided to make its four walls its life conquest kept us clear.

The house sat in between the pond, which could better be described as a small lake, and the field out front. Adjacent to the house to the east was the garage, and there was a smaller pond to the west.

This house was the place of frog croaks at night, dragonfly sightings by day, and infinite possibility by way of imagination. And imagination is the only three of those things that still exists within my reality today. So it's what I'll run with.

As much as the property of this particular home has remained in my mind, it is the series of ponds the property sat on that have captured my attention since the house left my family's ownership.

The only neighbor on the pond which my Nonnie and Papa lived on was an older widowed woman. She had been living there with her now-deceased husband since the property was purchased back in the 1960s by my great-grandfather. She and her husband bought up a large amount of property on this particular pond and others around it.

The area itself is known as Seven Ponds. The family that lived across from my grandparents was integral in donating land and money to build a nature center on the fifth pond of the seven. Seven Ponds Nature Center highlights midwestern flora and fauna. They have painted turtles, a turtle native to the region, in aquariums for visitors to study. There is a chalkboard logging different bird sightings that have happened in the area, and a makeshift beaver dam that kids can crawl into.

. . .

The trails make their way through the deciduous forest of the area with wooden walkways going over reeds and cattails around the ponds. There's a dock where you can see some of the bluegill and bass if you concentrate hard enough as you look into the water. And you'll be greeted by the dragonflies on your walks and the humming of cicadas.

The trails at Seven Ponds are the perfect embodiment of a southeastern Michigan nature experience.

And even if only three or so of the ponds can be seen from the nature center, the reason for the title of Seven Ponds is pretty self-explanatory—there are seven altogether. Some are more like lakes, some glorified swamps, but they all are a part of the whole.

My grandparents lived on the last of the seven. The most private of all of them. It would be rare that you'd see anyone but the people who lived on the other side of the pond or my family on this particular one of the seven. The occasional exception would be fishermen in canoe- sized boats. But all the pontoons and speedboats of the biggest of the seven ponds, the second in the series, rarely ventured this way.

It was all subtly serene. Even the water snakes, slicing through the water with their slithering, seemed to be just another byproduct of the place.

The Voice of the Ponds

Around the same time that I discovered the Pacific Northwest on Google Earth, I looked into finding places of familiarity as well. I zoomed into my family's neighborhood and my school and the hockey rink I played at.

I also zoomed in on Seven Ponds.

And the one thing that wasn't all that clear from the pixelated pictures of 2005 satellite imagery was the fact that each pond wasn't a stand-alone body of water, but that they were connected to each other by narrow canals.

The canals that we would honk into before entering with our boat to alert others making their way through. The little slivers of water with walls of cattails and reeds. The conduit's that connected the ponds of beers and barbeque to quiet and serenity.

You couldn't see these canals from the satellite imagery.

Seven Ponds has become a bit of a muse for me because of this connectedness they share. And, apparently, it's only a connectedness you know about when you encounter the reality in person. Which is fitting. Because I think the reality of that interconnectedness is a good metaphor for the idea of spiritual development, or development in general. And that type of thing isn't something theorized or viewed online, but happens tangibly.

Life starts in the busier part of the ponds, with bustle and BBQs, and eventually its makes its way to the quiet and reserved pond of my Nonnie and Papa. In this final place, where we may have one other neighbor, we've made our stake. Our ten acres of land is our definition of self. This definition took time to create; we had to make our way out of the bustle and through the loneliness to reach this place. But now we're here.

And here is a place of infinite familiarity. The frogs croaking out the window of my grandparents' house were what led to a restful night of sleep. The turtles poking their heads out of the water were the image of curiosity. The dragonflies that would swirl around on the dock were wonder, in insect form. The wooded borders of the land represented the familiarity of the unfamiliar.

Everyone is working toward a lake house in their life, I think. A sense of place, not necessarily literal, but a state in which *belonging* can be the only accurate term. And in my experience, the places where we feel we belong most are those places where the thought of belonging is the furthest from our minds. Because in those places, we just are. Simply and truly.

But it takes time to get there. Because between the big pond near the beginning of the series of seven and my grandparents' pond are a few ponds of relatively small size. Then, also off the main, big pond in the opposite direction is a murky pond that appears to be more like a swamp. In hindsight, I see the big pond as society or collective identity in general. A place where we all start, with so many options and possibilities of trajectory. The swamp is what happens when we get crippled by a multitude of possibility so great that we can't seem to go anywhere but a place of being stuck. But in the other direction there's the option to venture through the canal that leads to one of the smaller ponds that lie between the main pond and the last of the seven.

These in-between ponds are lonely. There's not much in them, and not many people spend any amount of time there. But through the process of self-discovery and pressing on amidst the unfamiliar, you eventually reach the last pond of the seven. A place of identity. Of self-actualization big enough to explore but not so overwhelming that you get lost.

The idea of progress is one that begs us to break away from ingrained thought and into personal identity. And this is lonely. But there's nothing better than hearing frogs ushering you into sleep, or gravel driveways where you can find fossils millions of years old. Progress is always a difficult process. But the yield self-discovery gives way for is always worth the pursuit.

Revelations on Target Toilets

As much as I would have liked to give myself over to the way of selfless love the underground river spoke to, my mind, while at Moody, was largely in a place of taking in theory rather than living it out. Even in the writing and blogging that was transpiring, I still lived more in theory than in practice, and this theory didn't really know where it would continue to grow after my freshman year at Moody. So that next summer was difficult. I felt trapped in a canal, you could say.

I had visited Whitworth University, also in Spokane, in January of my freshman year at Moody. Whitworth had hundreds of ponderosa pines, black lanterns lining the sidewalks, and, the day I visited, a white blanket of snow on the ground. The only thing missing was Mr. Tumnus, and it would've been like I had just walked through the wardrobe. I loved Whitworth. And on YouTube, I had seen that they had brought in Peter Rollins to speak a couple of years prior.

Whitworth seemed like a place that engaged in theology but also a place that was more open to exploration in such areas. And as a liberal arts school, it seemed like there would be an opportunity to learn from a lot of different disciplines.

On top of that, the natural setting of Whitworth is the cliché picture of college that you see in movies growing up. There are brick buildings everywhere, and a central loop littered with ponderosa pines. Every building is within a five-to-ten-minute walk, and on the walk from one building to the next, you're bound to be smiled at and have to dodge a few frisbees. It's almost laughable how peaceful of a place it is. It was voted the third-friendliest Christian school in the country while I attended, and in the top twenty for most beautiful.

Whitworth was founded in 1890 in western Washington. In 1914, Whitworth moved over to Spokane, which is on the eastern side of the state. Whitworth is a relatively small liberal arts school. About 2,300 undergraduate students were enrolled during my time there. Because of the small size, Whitworth has an underlying pulse tied to the idea of community. Whitworth loves this word. By the time you graduate, you want to gag every time you hear it. But like my, and so many of my peers' experience postgrad, you long for it when it's gone. Because there really is a sense that you are known at this place.

The student to faculty ratio is about twelve-to-one. Small classes, an abundance of office hours, and kind-hearted people lead to professor and student dynamics that make

Mitch Albom's friendship with his professor Morrie in his book *Tuesdays with Morrie* seem like the norm.

During my snow-filled visit, I sat through an admissions presentation only to have my hopes crushed by the $50,000 price tag. I was assured the price would go down with financial aid, only to be crushed a second time when I saw an admissions percentage hovering just above 50 percent. My grades were about on par with, well, a course whose par is a 2.7 GPA. Academic drive and I weren't the most familiar of friends.

My plan was to go home to Michigan for the summer, run some phone and internet cable with my dad's friend, Tom Stone, do some gardening for family friends, and then come back to Spokane to attend community college for a year, then transfer to Whitworth after I got my GPA up. This plan was received with cynicism.

"Mikey, you're not going to go to community college 2,000 miles away from home. Why would you do that? You have free housing here," my Dad said, which inspired an agreeing nod of approval from my mother.

He had a good point. It did seem rather ridiculous. But what seemed even more ridiculous to me was giving up and coming back to everything I had ever known after only a year of living away from home. I saw myself sitting shotgun with Mr. Stone on my off days of school at a community college back in Michigan, running foot upon foot, yard upon yard, mile upon mile, of cable. And I heard my high school psychology teacher's words in my head, patronizing those who never end up living for much time outside of a ten-mile radius from where they grew up. And I still wanted to have theoretical conversations about theology, even if they were with Moody friends like Jake and Adam who found my ideas crazy at times. And I kept seeing the satellite images of the Pacific Northwest I had fallen in love with on Google Earth eight years previous.

I just wasn't ready to give it up.

And then, as I sat on a toilet in Target, it became apparent that I wouldn't have to give it up; I had just felt the buzz of an email. And this particular email told me I had been accepted to Whitworth.

I found my mom. She got super excited. I was nervous about tuition cost, but she said we'd work it out. And low and behold we did (yay for crippling student loan debt!), along with some grant help from Whitworth. Come late August, I was boarding a plane to head back to the Pacific Northwest.

An Ideological Mess

Something interesting happens when you live existentially for too long. You forget about the ground you walk on. And when you forget about the ground you walk on, you forget that any idea worth its salt is one that allows you to take steps. Progress. And move toward something. And also is an idea that is centered around dirt... but we'll get to that later.

By the time I headed back out to Spokane to begin at Whitworth, I was in a frame of mind ready to encounter something different than Moody, but in a frame of mind largely lost within the frame of theoretical thought, as opposed to actual existence.

I lived within a frame of ideology that worked to rid itself of any and all expectations. I firmly believed that if I didn't expect anything from a situation, person, or experience, I would experience everything exactly as it was supposed to be experienced. And, if there were no expectation tied to anything, then everything would exceed the (nonexistent) expectation. But, as is the problem when living theoretically and not actually, my theory didn't find stable ground.

As my future friend and mentor Mindy Smith would later tell me, every idea that wants to become a reality needs legs. And the legs to ideas typically are found in the reality of the world, a place I didn't spend all that much time living in during this phase. Instead, I played the role of Gollum, the famous *Lord of the Rings* cave dweller, searching for meaning in the inner caverns of my mind.

Upon entering Whitworth, I looked for places to experience liberation from the grasp of rules Moody had put on my collegiate educational career. This liberation proved to be easier to find than expected. The first time I met my roommate that year he was high on DMT, a hallucinogen occurring naturally in all living things, released during dreams and death, but occurring naturally in him after a couple of deep breaths accompanied by some smoke. The first time I met him, he queued me in on his newly acquired ability to hear color. Such a giant leap of liberation into the land of potent hallucinogenic drugs seemed a bit too far of a leap for me, and my intrigue was only lived out through asking questions.

But I did take more steps back in that direction. It wasn't all that long before our room smelled like marijuana twenty-four-hours a day. And this stench was not solely my roommate's fault. In those days, inspired in part by Washington's legalization of weed, I saw no moral dilemma in smoking. Which, even now, I see no problem with, at the proper age and within the proper state lines. And, most importantly, with the right frame of mind attached to the motivation for it. I, however, had no such frame within my little brain at the time. The smoking and occasional (over) drinking that was tied to my life during this phase was a coping mechanism for a lonely place known as my thoughts.

After leaving Moody, I had generated a lot of ideas. These ideas swirled, hopped, and played around in my mind. But the mind isn't what hugs, shakes the hand of, or high fives another. Authenticity is what plays that role.

The beginning of my sophomore year saw difficulty in the realm of authenticity. Largely because of my obsession with being authentic. Mike Christie had become an idea, a concept. I wanted to be shaped by a persona of intrigue, intellect, and oddball idiosyncrasies.

Such longed-for traits were manifested through spouting off the theories existing in my mind, wanting to be released so I could find space to breathe—

"I'm a Christian atheist."
"I'm a Christian Nihilist."
"I don't hold any expectations."

These phrases I'd spew were philosophies so convoluted and heady that the only way they found any life was attaching themselves to my breath as I said them. It was really fascinating. But also, quite lonely.

But Whitworth wasn't all wacky and weird wonderings for the neurons. Fairly quickly after starting there came the excitement that comes with a new setting. There was living in a coed dorm rather than a single-showered house with eight guys. There was meeting new friends. There were the nights of sneaking in the music building with Alex, Bryson, Brayden, and Luke. Luke playing violin, Brayden playing viola, and me playing guitar; Bryson spilling fireball on pianos, Alex grooving in painfully uncomfortable sways, and all of us singing in the most brutal of falsettos. There was all of that. And it was all coupled with a mix of wanting to be authentic to ideas yet becoming fake through multiple acts that were used to mask my avoidance of living out those ideas.

What You Do with Your Breath

The Hebrew word for God is Yahweh. Or at least that's how it's spelled so we can pronounce it. One way to understand the translation is simply the letters YHVH. These four letters, when pronounced in the Hebrew language, are the sound you make when you breathe. Rob Bell has a video on this called Breathe if you want it further explained.

So, that being said, when you breathe, you are uttering the name of God. That, combined with the fact that the Hebrew word for breath and the word for the spirit of God are the same word, *ruach*, makes it quite obvious that God is as near as every breath. Or perhaps even resides in every breath we take.

The irony of it all is that I had a lot of theories about God, but didn't realize that who or what God was happened to be entering and exiting my lungs with every theory that I spouted off, every falsetto I let ring out, and interwoven in every hit I took. The difficult thing is the theories, falsettos, and hits were all my attempt to feel something, and also the distractions taking me away from the present. The very place I needed to be to feel this mystical presence that was as close as my very breath.

But music was still a place of authenticity for me. It was in music that my personality found an escape from my pain-in-the-ass self. And it was music that led me to meet my wife.

Emily and the Death of Sacrificial Jesus

If The Mowgli's were my ticket to feeling a sense of just how interconnected the cosmos were (more on that later), Death Cab for Cutie was a consistent source allowing me to feel how empty my soul was. And so, naturally, it was a concert for the front man on Death Cab, Ben Gibbard, that led me to spend time with the girl who, at first, would empty my soul like no other. But, with time, would fill my soul to a place of overflow. Much like the elusive Death Cab lyric from "Marching Bands of Manhattan"

Sorrow drips into your heart through a pinhole. Just like a faucet that leaks, there is comfort in the sound. And as you debate whether half empty or half full, it slowly rises, your love is going to drown.

I knew I would marry Emily Fisher in December of 2014, even if she would reject my initial attempts at dating the following month. And even if she would not actually say yes to a date until January of 2016—as they say, sometimes, you just know.

Every young heart is a soldier fighting for its cause. My heart had to suffer through a few stabs that included excruciating twists of the knife. I had the memory of said marital knowledge written down on a Word document on my computer. It read something to the effect of: Although I can't travel back in time like they can in *About Time* (we had just watched that movie together), an awareness stirred in me tonight that makes me wish I could. Because tonight, Emily Fisher, is the night I knew I would be reading this note to you on a very special day.

Lofty, wasn't it?

And so, as promised, just over two years later I would read Emily that note on one knee while overlooking the shores of the lake I discovered on Google Earth back in fifth grade that led me out to this part of the country.

It's interesting how something like this note, if Emily were to have happened upon it a day after I wrote it, could have been perceived as quite creepy. But, when read at the right time, could be seen as some bizarre and unexplainable piece of a cosmic love story. This, ironically enough, is the same way one has to push through the frustration and jargon of spirituality, in order to see it in a new and beautiful light. The same things can evoke wildly different responses depending on the timing.

But before any of this, there was rejection.

When I met Emily, and during the trip we took early on with

her roommate Ashley to the Ben Gibbard show, I was not in any place to be falling in love.

And yet, as these things tend to go, I was falling in love.

Emily was unlike any girl I had ever been around. She was peaceful, beautiful, and held a presence of something my idea-occupied mind knew nothing of at the time—ease. There was a lightness to her. She, as I would later tell her, and still say today, was someone who made everything matter.

Not matter in a theoretical sense like my mind was used to at the time but in a tangible sense. Emily made my mind come back to the place of the material, and recognize how much more beautiful that can be than the place of theory. Especially when the material played host to a girl as wonderful as her.

But the difficulty that happens when you meet someone who can shift your psyche is you inevitably take the idolatrous nature of the psyche you are currently in, and place it all on that person or thing. They, or it, become your out. And what is at first pure heaven and freedom and liberation becomes the very victim of the obsessive mindset you (in this case I) had been in. Emily was falling victim to the idolatrous nature of one-sided love. And she had every reason to deny me because of it.

Given the precarious nature of my live-through-theory plagued situation, I began to think that I needed Emily. And I had all the theory that backed up why! Her pure and Christ-like ways were, in my mind, the ticket I needed as an out from the fake persona I had been living in.

As any young romantic has to learn when love is framed as *I need you*, very little freedom is left for the person who is supposedly needed to exist as themselves.

Ironically, what I needed was a chance to uncover why I felt I needed Emily. Which, because paradox always is where truth resides, is what the blessing of rejection ultimately yielded.

Emily wanted to go for a walk. We had watched *Good Will Hunting* the night before, and things seemed a bit off. There wasn't a spark, and this is exactly what Emily told me on said walk. Through this rejection my mind could begin to move to a place not of *I need you* but to the place of *I never knew I needed you, but now that you are in my life, now that I've experienced you truly as yourself, I want nothing more than continuing my life with you.*

. . .

Love, I found through reflection after this process, should never be based on a predetermined, preexisting, presumed paradigm of needs. Rather, love has to call into existence a whole new paradigm you never thought possible. Which requires the painful process of ridding oneself of the present paradigm one resides within.

Which, of course, takes us to why God *didn't* need Jesus to die on the cross. An idea that is in paradox to the dominant narrative of western Christianity, which seeks to say Jesus died on the cross to save you from your sin and, ultimately, hell. Which to me always seemed like a masked way of saying that Jesus died on the cross to save you from... God. Because is it not God who makes the choice to send a sinner to hell?

Just as romantic love doesn't exist within the scope of existing paradigms, but rather in the creation of a whole new paradigm, so too is the case for Divine love. At least that's what I'm inclined to believe...

One difficulty I had to face at Moody was the overwhelming idea people around me seemed to hold of the need to be "covered in the blood of Jesus." Not only was such an idea rather gross to imagine, but it also seemed contrary to the idea of renewal that the *blood of Jesus* ultimately led to in resurrection.

The narrative for this form of Christianity that my peers at Moody adhered to saw Jesus as the *ultimate sacrifice*. Jesus was seen as, to use a common Christian metaphor, the lamb that, through dying, took away the weight of sin for humanity.

But, in this theological understanding my peers had, in order for that sin to be gone, Jesus had a caveat. You still had to accept that Jesus did that for you. In this light, Jesus seemed awfully like a kid who did something nice on the playground solely for the perk of being seen as nice. And, if not seen as nice, that same kid, in this case Jesus, would turn their back on the ones he had just been nice to.

On top of that, being covered in the blood of something dead seemed pretty contrary to the idea of spreading new life to dead places, the very idea Jesus' life seemed to be all about. It just seemed like a reminder of death death DEATH.

The paradigm within Jewish thought, which was the paradigm of thought that Jesus was within, had been one of death to begin with. Or, more specifically, a paradigm of sacrifice.

But it seemed that in the Bible, God was always working people towards new paradigms, not keeping them in old ones. And, because God is love and love requires new paradigms, it seemed obvious that the paradigm of sacrifice had to be left behind for something new. And, in that light, this newness couldn't be the need for yet another sacrifice. Which in this case would have been the sacrifice of Jesus, like the theology around me suggested. Because that's just the same old paradigm.

And if a headstrong sophomore in college like me could understand love necessitating the need for a new paradigm, it seemed logical to me that the breath, wind, and spirit of the cosmos could also recognize this need. I didn't believe that it was a "sacrifice" that Jesus was dying for. I think it was an act trying to get us to recognize that sacrifice wasn't what God was longing for. God wanted to reveal something else. A new paradigm.

Around the time that Emily rejected me was also around the time that my opinion of God's love began to find new life. Which, in the long run, was what led me out of my funk and into a place of personal identity again.

I had begun to understand the necessity for love creating

new paradigms, as I've mentioned, which led me to understand the necessity of Jesus *not* being a sacrifice. Because if he was a sacrifice, that wasn't love. That was redundancy. The redundancy of something that hadn't worked for the psyche of the Jewish people for thousands of years. And, just as Elon Musk is said to have kicked people out of his boardroom whose reasoning for doing something is because that's the way it has always been done, God seems to leave people with mindsets stuck in past paradigms at a loss with God's natural bent toward progress and expansion. God, like Musk, is about new dynamics – the expansion of thought rather than redundancy. Pushing forward as opposed to clinging to the past.

Sacrifice was the same old dead end the Bible always led to. It's what it's lost little characters always seemed inclined to pursue. And sacrifice can be good when it is seen as a way of putting others before self, but when it's to appease or gain some end in return, it missed the point. What I discovered, with the help of many other theologians I was reading at the time, was that when you look at the Bible as a work of progress, you see that God was, and is, not mad and in need of blood to be appeased. But instead was, and is, strongly insisting just how much love was, and is, a part of whatever God has been doing all along. No sacrifice required.

As Richard Rohr beautifully puts it, it wasn't God's mind Jesus was trying to offer a new paradigm to as he hung on the cross, but mine and yours and all the Jews stuck in a mindset revolving around the sacrificial system. God had been all along trying to instill the recognition that *the good news* is not recognizing our supposed inability and repenting over and over again. Instead, the *good news* is simply knowing you're enough without having to think about why.

Because that's the very nature of love. Knowing it's existence or presence or embrace of you, even if you don't understand it.

It was this new paradigm that wound up allowing me to love me for myself. It was no longer about what I did and did not do, but about who I was and am.

This new paradigm also led me, through the course of a year truly leaning into this truth, to be in a place to love Emily for who she was, not who I needed her to be. Sacrifice is all about God forcing us to be who or how God needs us to be.

But that's not the story God is telling.

How God needs us to be is in oneness with the earth, living in coexistence just as we were in the creation poem located in Genesis. God is all about us letting things be what they are and discovering the harmony tied to that reality. And a reality of harmony and oneness is certainly not a reality in need of sacrifice.

Washington Capitals

Sports are fascinating. And they were a dominant part of my life growing up. When I went to college, I made friends with a lot of people who just didn't get it. The passion behind sports that I had seemed funny or odd or like grabbing at something intangible. They didn't understand the contrast of agony and euphoria that accompanies rooting for a team.

But pulling for a team always made sense to me. Pulling for a collective group over another is arguably the most historically accurate depiction of human nature we have.

It's the tribe mentality, your tribe against mine. No different than the Spartans against the Athenians, the Persians against the Greeks, the Romans against the Huns, the Americans against the Russians. From the dawn of time, tribes fight other tribes. The winner gets pride; the loser gets shame.

The psychology of sport is the psychology of competing

cultures. And now instead of spears and guns (although those things still exist, sadly) we have tackling and hip checks. Home runs and touchdowns. We try to make the Olympics peaceful, but what if we used them as the place where all foreign relations could be solved, winners and losers, based on the results of the events? We'd likely have a lot less war. And yet the overarching theme would remain the same—I win, you lose.

Sports, like anything that allows you to tie yourself to something bigger than yourself, are beautiful. But also, just like anytime you place hope in something you can't control solely on your own but desperately long for, sports can be absurdly painful.

Societal comparisons aside, this overdrawn reading of sports is not the way I interact with them normally. I grew up playing them, predominantly hockey and golf. For someone who is an overthinker in every aspect of life, sports were the place my mind turned off.

In hockey, I would skate hard every shift.

In golf, I would hone in, focus, and visualize.

But the harbor for my athletically inclined mind is now almost strictly based on fandom. And that fandom is largely tied to a single entity.

When I was in sixth grade, I adopted something into my life. It wasn't Jesus. It wasn't a puppy. It wasn't a brother or a sister.

It was a curse.

And that curse was a fandom for the NHL team that calls our nation's capital home. There are many different cases to be made for the hardest sports team to root for. Prior to 2016, the case was probably best made for the Chicago Cubs. Going a century without a championship is a bit hard to top. Think of the people who, every year, put on their Cubs gear, only to time and time again be left with disappointment. Brutal.

But they won the world series recently, so all is well.

I read an article about the most difficult teams to root for. It was a bit dated, but most of the teams listed were ones with a poor record around the time it was written. My hometown Detroit Lions were ranked second given their, at the time of the article, recent record of zero wins and sixteen losses. But as painful as it is to watch your team win zero games for a season, there is, at least, the recognition six or so games into the season that your team will likely amount to nothing.

What's worse, I would argue, are teams that show promise year in and year out, only to completely crumble when it matters most. Like the armies of old with all the might needed to win any battle, only to be defeated in utter embarrassment. And although I'm willing to hear cases of teams who fit this mold more, I think you'd be hard-pressed to find a team more difficult to pull for in the last ten years than the Washington Capitals.

And the Capitals are precisely who I've chosen to pull for throughout that stretch of time.

It all began with the introduction of the Russian phenom, Alexander Ovechkin. He burst onto the scene, winning the Rookie of the Year award and putting up over fifty goals his first season—I was hooked. The Capitals slowly became an offensive juggernaut in the late 2000s. They were putting up more goals than thought possible in the new, lower scoring, dynamic of the NHL. Since I became a fan, they've won the Presidents' Trophy, as the NHL's best regular season team, three times, and have made the playoffs nine times.

And they haven't made it past the second round of the playoffs once in that span. The NHL has four rounds in its postseason. Not once out of the second.

Hockey playoff series are based on a best four out of seven series. A game seven in the Stanley Cup Playoffs is like nothing else in the world. It's truly a game of inches. Each movement of the puck sets your nerves on edge. The Capitals have played in ten of these games since I've been a fan. And they've lost seven of those ten.

The Capitals' rival, the Pittsburgh Penguins, the team with my nemesis, Sidney Crosby, have played the Capitals three times in the playoffs since I've become a fan. The Capitals have won zero of those series. On top of that, each time the Penguins beat the Capitals in the playoffs, the Penguins went on to win the Stanley Cup.

The Capitals are a painful team to root for.

So why bother? Every year when the playoffs end the same way they do in years past, I vow that I'm done. That I'm not going to watch them anymore. And yet, as early October rolls around, you'll be hard-pressed to find me anywhere but on a couch watching their first game of the season.

I'm like a dog returning to its vomit.

. . .

But maybe what this fandom speaks to is actually quite beautiful.

There's a special kind of hope tied to it.

Hope that things will be different. Hope that this time, things will change.

Hope that this will be the year.

Can you imagine if people who relentlessly stay with a sports team year in and year out, even after season upon season of failure, applied that approach to every time someone said they weren't good enough. That they should give up. That they should settle. That they aren't capable. If we applied the same level of commitment and dedication to our own beliefs about who we are and what we are capable of, that we do to our sports teams, we'd likely become exactly what we dream of becoming.

Or what about applying that level of hope and loyalty to all the people who have let us down? What if we showed them the same level of commitment as we show our teams? Failure after failure we always come back to support them.

It doesn't mean when there's a let down that you can't be mad or upset about it. I've shattered glasses that I threw across the room when the Capitals lost. It just means that you come back to the hope, relentlessly believing in possibility. That's something we need to do more of, I think. Relentlessly believe in possibility. Because whatever it is, a Stanley Cup Championship or publishing your first book or giving someone another chance, the good will happen eventually if you stick with it.

In the meantime though, feel free to throw a glass or two.

*As of June 7, 2018, the Capitals are Stanley Cup Champions. And guess what? They beat the Penguins in the second round.

Oh how sweet it is.

People Need Their Own Words

During my sophomore year of high school, I organized games of pick up pond hockey at Beverly Park, which was about a mile away from where I lived. Over time, the games turned into a pretty huge hit. On the weekends, we'd get around twenty or thirty guys to show up and play. Each one of us took our turn rotating into the four-on-four chaos. In a desperate attempt to find ice time, the brave ones played goalie and had their ankles shot at with vulcanized rubber, inevitably leading to blood. Jawing at each other was the norm. There were plenty of chances to give chewing tobacco a try, with some of the older guys packing lips with the disgusting tar. My parents would swing by with pizza while we played for hours.

It was a 16-year-old's paradise.

Some of us were skilled skaters with good hands, weaving in and out of the others who tumbled all over the pond and couldn't seem to stand upright, stickhandling the puck on the cracked surface as if it was nothing. And then others had to create a third leg, via hockey stick. Placing all of their weight on the stick for support, looking like an old cartoon character dancing as they tried to find balance.

But come spring the ice would thaw and turn into a puddle, and what once was tangible to skate on, what had been a steady, albeit slippery, surface, was now fluid.

. . .

Water has three states—ice, liquid, and vapor. All three states are the same thing, just drastically different. Hockey only works on ice. It only works on what we can grasp. And even still, there are people with different skills and training that make interacting with the ice a varying process.

I grew up playing hockey, which means I spent a lot of time on ice, both on the pond and in warehouses. Ice is slippery and solid and all over the place and confusing. Ice is the solid and stationary state of water. Yet even in being stationary, ice still seems hard to gain traction with.

This in mind, ice is pretty much the perfect metaphor for the person of Jesus.

. . .

Recently, I was sitting around thinking, sucking a blueberry Jolly Rancher, as one does. And I realized that the Trinity, that whole Father, Son, and Spirit deal in Christian theology, hold characteristics remarkably similar to ice, liquid, and vapor.

Jesus is ice.
Father is liquid.
Spirit is vapor.

Which pairs well with some other words I have for this tri-divinity idea within Christianity.

Jesus as Existence.
Father as Insistence.
Spirit as Persistence.

Just as ice is a solid state, something we can grasp, Jesus was a physical existence.

But just as the ice on the pond can be slippery, and some of us can stumble while some of us seem to get it, Jesus was someone who seemed very against the idea of uniform takeaways upon interaction.

And just as the water of a river flows in a certain way, in a certain direction, with a certain aim, the insistence of God the Father, the overarching reality of whatever this Divinity throughout history is, pesters us to join in that same natural progression. It's wild and all over the place and moving with varying paces.

Just read any sacred historical text, and you'll see this if you look at it as a story steadily revealing itself.

And then there's vapor. Vapor is anywhere and everywhere without us always being aware of it. Vapor is always, in some way, even if invisible, there. Persisting us to recognize it. Like the Spirit in those moments of profound divine encounter, you can't really explain it. But it's bringing new life and refreshment to places that are parched and dry. Even if you can't see or know how.

When I had this idea, this whole three states of water idea, I thought I had come up with a whole new way to grasp the Trinity! It was huge! Profound! And I couldn't wait to tell someone, and so I did, and then—

"Oh yeah, that's really neat! Someone came and used that description once when I was in Sunday school. Not as detailed as yours obviously but I thought it was really cool!"

Ego. Shattered.

What I thought was this profound new insight into the three and one confusion of Christianity was a Sunday school illustration. And typically, when you hear that an idea or understanding you have is elementary, you can tend to walk away from it because of the shame you feel from thinking it was some profound insight.

But there is another option. And that's recognizing that every idea, no matter where it comes from or how it started, is a path you may need to keep walking down. So, I kept walking down this path, and I loved it, and now I use this idea all the time.

A fear of being unoriginal can often be the greatest curse to being original. Five people can look at the same painting and have a different takeaway. In the same light, billions of people can come to the same concept, say in this case, God. But their individual stories and what they do with the concept is what makes way for the beautiful reality of uniqueness.

So I think about the Trinity as water. Frozen Jesus. His flesh as compressed form like, the molecules of water when bonded together. But just as he never gives a straightforward answer, ice is unpredictable. And then there's the "Father" revealed in liquid; wild and crashing and falling and flowing, waiting for us to hop in and float on the fluidity that is divine awareness. And then the Spirit, that unattainable, invisible, yet ever-present vapor. Hydrating and giving life to us even when we are unaware.

. . .

I looked up the Trinity water analogy after I told Emily about it. Partially out of insecurity and partially because I wanted to learn about what people had to say about it. And irony, as it has a habit of doing, struck. The top article on the topic was how the metaphor was heretical. Because the Trinity is Father, Son, and Spirit all at once, and water can't be all the same things at the same time.

Please tell me you see my eyes rolling right now.

The whole idea of God having three different characteristics seems to be a pretty clear clue that one should probably avoid putting parameters on how God operates. Water can exist in three states at once because water is not limited to one location. There can be vapor in one place, ice in another, and liquid elsewhere. The person crying heresy was a person who focuses on the particular. God is literally everywhere and anywhere God wants to be.

God is not a specific molecule, but the concept of molecule itself.

So the words particular and parameter when paired with the word God don't exactly work

The main enemy of the metaphoric and poetic is often the particular and literal. And just as everyone's story starts with the particular but receives character through interaction, the particular is the doorway into the metaphoric. We should never stop at the particular if we are Jesus followers. Because it is Jesus who is always opening the door to metaphor. Just read anything he said.

We all need words for God, words that may have a concrete definition universally, yes. But also words that interact with our story in some intangible ways at first, words that take us to new realms. Because it's in those realms that God is waiting to say hello.

Anytime someone reworks their understanding of something, it is largely the language for that something that we have the hardest time reworking. This is because all words reflect something personal to us even if they are trying to speak to a universal concept.

When I say father, I think of my dad who has a monotone voice but has emotion coming out of him in the form of tears anytime he becomes proud. I think of the man who taught me how to play golf and hockey and to respect other people. When I say father, or hear father, I have a comfortable place for my mind to reside.

But there are people I know whose fathers abused them in horrific ways. When they hear God referred to as Father, their paradigm isn't full of love or proud tears or golf; it's full of pain and isolation and fear. One of the most intriguing things about language is how the same titles can evoke very different ideas.

When I began to have new realizations about God, my language for God also had to shift. And this led to an increasing amount of eye rolls from friends over the next few years. And those eye rolls came predominantly from people who had had a good foundation of God and often found no reason to walk away from words like Father, Spirit, and Son. Which is okay! And even if those words do evoke pain or turmoil for many, it's also important to recognize how beautiful it is that something as seemingly far-reaching as a deity could be labeled with such personal language. A Father, a Son, and Spirit which, when interpreted correctly, means a *breath*.

However, even after this well-intended defense of such titles attributed to God, around the time I was thinking about all this, I was in a phase where the words weren't working for me. Not at the fault of my dad or anything like that, but because they had gained so much baggage from places like Moody. And so, around the time that my understanding of what the dominant idea of Christianity, the Trinity, meant to me, I figured I also had the freedom to come up with completely different vernacular for the Trinity myself.

I am not some innovator in this area. People have been wrestling to make sense of how something like an often understood to be single figurehead of *God* could also be three different personas. So, people come up with their own language and new descriptions.

Recently, such a practice was made widely popular by Paul Young in his international bestseller, *The Shack*. Young came to my church at the same time I was interning, so I was able to meet and talk with him about this very idea during my senior year of college, two years after I had reworked my Trinity wording.

In *The Shack*, Young personified God as a black woman named Papa, relayed the Holy Spirit as an Asian woman with the name Sarayu, which means a soft, comforting, and relieving wind in Hindi, and named Jesus, rather unoriginally, I must say, Jesus. Young said for personal reasons and baggage he had tied to classical definitions, he needed to come up with new vernacular. As he put it matter-of-factly, "holy ghost isn't the most inviting terminology for something that's supposed to be residing inside you."

Spooky.

Young is a twenty-first-century Trinitarian genius, no matter what critics who push back against mainstream theological conversation may say. And that's because Young understands the necessity for Trinity in theology because of what theology without it has done. Like theology that has generated the bogus idea of God as a father needing to kill his son so this supposedly loving father can be with the rest of his children again. But he also recognizes the need to give some personal spice or flair to terms for the Trinity so they can hold the beautiful meaning intended for them. It's the same thing... just different.

Renaming the Divine Triplets

In reworking the Trinity, you are forced to rework not just the single term *God*, but three terms—*Father, Son, and Spirit*. And, as if the baggage that can be tied to one name isn't enough, when you tie three together, everyone, no matter how similar the doctrine they were raised with, brings in their own filters. Which leads to a new word pilgrimage! Sophomore year of college, that's what I did.

I went for walks alone, talked to my good friend, Elizabeth, in the basement of the dorm I lived in, listened to music and overanalyzed its lyrics, and discussed this new search for names with any and every person I had the slightest sense of relationship with. I was trying to come up with something new. And I wanted to hear what their words and metaphors were too.

Elizabeth was really into the sun. Not in a the-sun-is-so-nice-for-my-tan kind of way, but in a deeply spiritual way. She ended up getting a tattoo of the sun on her shoulder. The sun, to her, was a beautiful metaphor for God the Father.

Going on walks seemed to point toward the wind a lot because the wind would blow and I couldn't help but think about *ruach* over and over again when I felt it on my face. Ruach being the Hebrew word for spirit, wind, and breath. I interpreted every passing breeze as Spirit giving me a cold kiss.

Music was a whirlwind of mystery, in which there always seemed to be something insisting beyond the objectivity of a person's lyrics to the subjective nature of my personal experience.

And then there were more conversations I had with people I was close with that kept expanding the idea, and would for years to come.

Take for example a pastor and friend named Ryan I made junior year. Ryan uses the words lover, loving, and love to describe the Trinity as a whole.

My former boss and current friend, Dayna, uses the words heart, mind, and soul for her Trinitarian framework.

There have been so many different, unique takes on the Trinity that people have shared with me. And there are also takes or interpretations that I have tasted myself through present participation with the world. Father, Son, and Spirit could work, but I wanted to open up the floodgates to allow God to become more of a three-way theme than a set of three categories.

. . .

For me, this time of rephrasing came amidst reading about how God, or the Father part of the Trinity, didn't actually exist. At least according to the king of existential rabbit holes, Peter Rollins. I was sitting in the coffee shop at Whitworth, reading Rollins' new book at the time, The Divine Magician. He was analyzing a thought by Jack Caputo. And Caputo had his idea after reading some philosophy by the pain-in-the-ass-to-truth philosopher, Jacques Derrida.

Derrida, through Caputo, through Rollins, and right into my brain, was talking about the idea I began this whole tangent of a chapter with. The idea that words generate association with concepts. But the problem is that those concepts hold different associations that are distinctly personal for each of us. And how, when one tries to use any specific word to describe God, it's impossible to point at anything that can tangibly exist within that framework because of all the different connotations and images the word God generates in the minds of individuals.

Upon reading this, I set my phone down, smiled at someone, took a sip of coffee, and plummeted my hands into my backpack, looking for Aleve because my head hurt.

I read some more. The claim being made was that God as a concrete concept couldn't exist. Just as my expectation of who someone was supposed to be couldn't exist in partnership with the freedom and fluidity of who that person actually was. All reality was dependent on interaction with that reality, not dependent on some type of preconceived definition of something.

This resonated.

But, just because God as a concrete, singular, defined character could not *exist*, did not mean that God couldn't *insist*. Because Insistence isn't some super version of a being or a firm concrete image, which is what the idea of God as Father tends to be. Instead, Insistence points to a theme that is superseding category, and instead insisting above the realm of any singular narrow definition. Because insistence is bigger than any one concept, it can be encountered through any and every definition. Just as light is not housed in one light bulb, light is separate from the houses we give it. Insisting through multiple houses at any given time. All reality is a conduit to the reality of this Insistent God.

God, in this light, is more of an insistent event that happens. And this event is housed at the intersection of our personal experience and the holistic happenings of the cosmos. And perhaps the most profound and vivid reality of that intersection is when Jesus came into the world. And it is also at that intersection of the personal and the wholistic where we have personal and mystical encounters with God.

This meant that although God was not all, God was part of all. Again, similar to light.

And it also meant that wind, and those songs, and the sun, and that creator, creating, created, and love, heart, mind, and Father were all viable definitions of God because God was insisting in all those places. But as soon as we say God *is* one of those things, we lose the ability to see God flowing through all of those things.

Does this make sense? It's a bit like saying love is _____.
Which we can't do. Because love takes many forms and is a
part of many stories. Love insists within dynamics more than
love exists as a tangible concept.

When we say "God is _____" we miss the reality of seeing
God insist through _____.

God as Insistence rather than existence points to the idea
that all language / experience / existence / music / event is a
conduit, between the Divine and us. And we all know this,
because we look at the stars and are moved in the same
way that we are when we have a two hour long
conversation with someone we love and cherish. Both are
spiritual, but neither has a monopoly of what *is* spiritual.
Because God, the concept surrounding what is spiritual,
doesn't exist, but insists through these things.

This whole realization made sense out of something that I
had struggled making sense of. I had felt God insisting in
that Starbucks when I heard The Head and the Heart song. I
had interacted with the Insistence of God as I sobbed on my
bed after the Athanasius lecture. Sitting on a surfboard in
the Pacific Ocean was full that Insistence.

Eating burrito bowls with Michael Vincze, talking about
heaven on earth.

Chatting with Israel Nebeker about all the themes of life on
a bridge overlooking the Spokane River.

Driving down Adams Road in July of 2015.

When I knew I would marry Emily.

While listening to Night Beds perform live in a chapel in Portland my junior year of college.

When I looked back at a picture of my friend Jimmy, that I had taken of him looking out at the Lone Cypress in Carmel, not knowing that his Dad had died fifteen minutes earlier.

This Insistence was in all of that. It was like that light from the fireflies in my backyard. So free and fluid and illuminating reality for me in ways of beauty I couldn't have imagined.

Insistence, or the invitation to enter into the divine reality of the world, helped me land from the turbulent flight of spiritual angst. And, because I was rather fond of the Trinity, I added two words to this Insistent God theory—Existence for Jesus, and Persistence for Spirit. I had my Father, Son, and Spirit. My Heart, Mind, and Soul. My Love, Lover, Loving. My Papa, Sarayu, Jesus. My water, vapor, and ice.

Insistence, Existence, Persistence.

A year or so later, I would add the word theme as my blanket statement for all of it. And, like any good story, living my life as the unfolding event that it is led to the characterization of that theme.

. . .

The narrator Hanta in the Bohumil Hrabal novel *Too Loud a*

Solitude says that any good book worth its salt always points up and out of itself. So, if you are to consider the Bible a good book, which to some it is THE Good Book, it's essential to acknowledge the themes it speaks to. Themes that aren't just real in it's pages, but real in the lives we all live. And my take is, the theme it points to more than all others is the idea of bringing life to dead spaces. And the terminology you use for that doesn't matter as much as the participation with it through observation, appreciation, and wonder.

Fireflies do no good trapped inside a jar. And God does no good trapped inside a book.

Listening to the Bell and the Rohr

Through my discovery of new language for the Trinity, some help from the lyrics to the song "The Beginning Song" by The Decemberists, and the unnaturally sunny winter of my sophomore year, I had come up for air from the abyss of Christian nihilism I had fallen into. Being in the pool, to begin with, had been caused by a shift from reading Rohr and Bell to Nietzsche and Rollins. Not to mention being rejected by Emily... All speed bumps to be sure.

And although Rollins helped with the whole Insistent shift, his book *The Divine Magician* left my head spinning. I was just finishing up my partial stint of atheism for Lent, which was another Rollins project of *giving up God* for a season and reading all the best critiques of religion. The project of giving up God is a beautiful one in some ways. It asks for participants to give up the notions of God that they believe in for the Lenten season and read some of the best atheist critiques of God. These critiques are wide-ranging, spanning from Karl Marx to Ludwig Feuerbach, and include critiques of rebuttals to said critique. And the beauty of this is that the things Christians, myself included, often repress are forced to the surface. I took it upon myself to attempt forcing those things to the surface for others.

It was good to get out of this headspace and instead experience the reality right in front of me again.

. . .

I went to a church called Vineyard 509 at this point. And had been going since I started at Moody. The community was full of love and grace and kindness. It was started by a husband and wife named Jason and Amber and their friends Kao and Tanya. They all were my family away from family in Spokane. Jason supported me a lot while at Moody. We had conversations about all the frustrations I had with what Moody taught. But Jason didn't really understand some of the more rabbit hole-esque theology I enjoyed. Namely, things I attributed to being nihilistic takes on Christianity.

Jason was an Easter person. I was a Good Friday person at the time. Basically, Jason was all about hope; I was all about acknowledging suffering. Two outlooks the wide-ranging spectrum of Christianity attempts to touch on.

Because of this, Jason graciously handed the production and implementation of the Good Friday service that year to me. And because I was being influenced by Nietzsche at the time and his "God is dead" ways, I decided the Good Friday service would be a good time to hold a funeral for Jesus.

I played songs about death and loss, and I wrote a poem eulogy for the fallen and supposed God. I had everyone write up their prayers and hopes on notecards and toss them in a wastebasket. Then, I poured lighter fluid on them, burnt them, and proclaimed that God was dead.

Easter, according to my spiritual angst, was too readily celebrated without the reality of the death that preceded it. And to truly appreciate new life, you also have to appreciate and acknowledge death.

The event was interesting, powerful, and pretty peculiar, but also made me ready for the new life of Easter. Ready for that breath of fresh air past the land of nihilism, Nietzche and nothingness. This fresh air had, ironically, accumulated in my lungs from the result of an email sent a few months previous while in the midst of the downer places.

. . .

In mid-December of 2014, I saw that Rob Bell was having a conference with Richard Rohr. And that the conference was to be held in the sunny land of Laguna Beach, California. I had heard of these conferences Bell put on before and had long been envious of them. Sunshine and surfing and theology were a soup my life wanted to slurp...

But I had no money.

But where there isn't money, there is pity. And so, I emailed a random email address I found on Bell's site, explained the "dire" situation of this broke college student and his longing to be at such an event, having read so much of both authors work. And, as luck or blessing or generosity would have it, I got an email back minutes later from Bell's agent telling me that he forwarded my email to Bell. And that Bell got back to him saying he wanted me to attend for free on a scholarship. Said scholarship included the two-day conference with Rohr and a single-day event the Wednesday after on creativity.

Queue a quick Expedia search for flights as a Christmas gift request, and I was set to go and learn from the two minds that helped me form this new scope of thought I had found freedom within.

One of the perks of this being the result of a scholarship was the wiggle room it gave me to miss four days of college classes. Come March, I headed down to southern California, my first excursion to the state of the sun, In-N-Out Burger, and endless coastal highways. Through connections with the Vineyard churches in the area that Jason had, I had a ride set up for when I got there. This ride was courtesy of a man named Don, who had a convertible. And as Don and I drove south from John Wayne Airport to Laguna, and as the Pacific Ocean crashed into the ridge to my right, and as he stopped at a local park to point out some whales breaching, I thought I had died.

This was too surreal.

. . .

I walked everywhere that week. A brand new pair of Rainbow flip-flops were run to the ground. Before going to the opening talk, I sat on the beach eating swordfish tacos.

The presence of waves breaking, sunshine, and palm trees was a literal shift of setting much like the theological shift of setting I underwent while at Moody with the help of Rohr and Bell's work.

This was a land of sun, Washington was a land of clouds. The openness of the theology this conference promised was the sun; the cloudiness was the closed-mindedness I had found so vile last year at Moody. The conference was also significantly better and more hopeful than the initial angst I used as a rebuttal to the closed-mindedness. There was an ease to this setting. And I hoped the conference would give ease to the, if slowly finding new trajectory, still relatively stiff stature of the theology within me.

Sufficiently satisfied by swordfish tacos, I wandered up the hill to the conference building. There were so many people! All were filtering into a room with chairs pointing in the direction of stained glass, two chairs up front, and a giant notepad. But this room wasn't just audience and act; it was warm, and not because of the California climate. I don't exactly know what or how or why, but there was an air of freedom and looseness, an unassuming air that filled the place.

These were mostly people who, I suspected but would later come to find out, had felt burned or bogged down by the church at some point or another. There were people here who had been told to be quiet about their sexual orientation, or quiet to the fact that they were being beaten at home, or that they couldn't preach because of their gender. People forced to repress or not live into their own actuality by conservative segments of the church. But here they felt safe. It was a place of profound humility and lightness.

I sat down three rows from the front, next to a woman named Dawn who was in her early seventies. She reminded me of my high school English teacher, Ms. Karolak. Dawn told me she had driven an hour and a half to be here. I told her I flew. She said she was here for Rohr; I said I was more familiar with Bell. And through our greeting of opposing realities, I immediately knew Dawn was a woman I wanted to be friends with.

I told her about my time at Moody, she told me about a painful previous religious dynamic and what sounded like a prior marriage that was part of its pain. Of feeling demeaned. Belittled. Incompetent.

Dawn and I were eager listeners of the spiritual teachers we came to see, nudging one another as Rohr and Bell would say something we felt would resonate with the other. We were a college kid and seventy-year-old woman nudging each other over assumed theological interest. Or perhaps more pointedly put, two people of varied paths to the place they now sat, elbowing at insights to new freedom they were living into and reminders of it. We grinned ear to ear as we chatted about the points being made during breaks, her trying to interpret my scribbled notes, adding her takeaways to them.

Dawn was a friend in the most heavenly sense.

There was a certain wonder and almost tear filled joy tied to the intertwined nature of seeing a whale breach and nudging a woman some fifty years older than me because of our shared giddiness for the freedom of open-minded spirituality. These two seemingly static events spoke to the same theme of beauty in the world being littered all around. The Insistence of a God with a trajectory of beauty and connectedness. It was so overwhelming and sunny and light. I don't really know what words to use. But beauty and hope and freedom were certainly there, Insisting that this place was *good*.

. . .

The entirety of the conference was incredible. I got to sit and listen to two of the greatest minds at the forefront of rethinking Christianity. On top of that, I met people like Dawn, a woman far older than me but working through the same reframing of faith. I got to meet Patrick Chappell, him and I got dinner together one night. We talked about the freedom of knowing you're not restrained by things you are *supposed* to believe. He is someone who to this day is one of the first places I turn to when it comes to talking about spirituality. He even ended up flying out to Washington to DJ my wedding. And there were countless others. Conversations over tacos and during breaks that were so resonate.

All this and there was only one duty asked of me because of the free access to it I had been given. And that was to sweep up the floor of the room the conference was in each night when Rohr and Bell were done speaking.

During this time of sweeping, I'd spend my time gathering all the different ideas presented to me into little piles in my mind, as I created little piles of dust on the floor. And these piles of ideas and thoughts would gain personality from the questions I would overhear individuals asking Bell or Rohr before they went on their way. Questions of how to deal with a spouse who may still see things different ways. Or parents who didn't agree with your way of living. Or friends who cut off ties from theological difference. My idea piles slowly acquired vital signs through the testimonies heard while the floor was being swept. I was forced to tie theory to reality.

Simple sweeping tied to eavesdropping peoples storys tied the miraculous and the common intimately.

The last night in California I was walking back to my hotel room when my phone rang. It was a number from the Los Angeles area, at least that's what caller ID led me to believe. I considered not answering, figuring it was a telemarketer and not wanting to ruin the sense of peace and growth I was marinating in. But I did.

"Hey Mike, it's Mike!"

Michael Vincze

I'm a band junkie. Or I guess, better said, I was a band junkie. I still am a bit, but not as much as I was in high school. At around the same time I was getting ready to go to Moody, and when I was reading Bell's book *What We Talk About When We Talk About God*, the book I mentioned earlier that was so pivotal for me, I discovered a band called The Mowgli's.

The best way I can describe them is sunshine rock. They were, at the time I fell in love with them, an eight-piece band. They joined all their voices together during choruses. They oozed out joy. They even went on a tour promoting random acts of kindness. The Mowgli's made feel good music.

They had one song in particular that I carried with me at Moody. Its chorus became my alternative doctrinal statement to differentiate my stance from the theological stance of the school. Here's what it says,

"I've been in love with love and the idea of something binding us together, you know that love is strong enough. I've seen time and heard tales of that systematic drug - that heat that beats as one - it's collectively, unconsciously composed."

For a kid whose main influences were Emerson, Thoreau, high school English teacher Sandra Karolak (think Emerson, Thoreau, and Mary Oliver, but still with a pulse), Christopher McCandless, Jesus, his mother, and Rob Bell, this chorus struck a chord. Because I had tapped into the reality it spoke to via all those people and ideas. And all those ideas transcended the minimal nature of any specific religious doctrinal statement like the one found at Moody.

One of my first escapades while at Moody was to drive to Seattle from Spokane over Labor Day weekend for Seattle's music festival, Bumbershoot. While there, sandwiched in-between eating a gyro drowning in tzatziki sauce and seeing Death Cab for Cutie play *Transatlanticism* in its entirety, I experienced the anthemic chorus of "San Francisco" live.

I view music as a guiding force telling me how to feel, when to feel, and why I feel a certain way. Which may not be the healthiest of tendencies, but that's just the reality. While listening to "San Francisco" in the Seattle sun with people bobbing up and down, I felt good, really good, because the setting was seeping with this authentic and oddly tangible sense of harmony.

This moment was spirit, church, holiness, whatever you wanted to call it. And it smelled like weed and burped up gyro.

Later that year, while home for Thanksgiving, a friend and I went to see The Mowgli's in Detroit. My friend's raffle ticket, which she got for donating canned food to a local nonprofit, was called, so we were able to go backstage and meet the band after the show. One of the main singers named Michael Vincze and I hit it off. I ranted to him about Moody and learned he had had similar experiences with fundamentalist faith. He told me about breaking out of the funk by interning for a Catholic priest who was a closet Buddhist. We were instantly friends. It was a match made in heaven. Or, to some of my school peers at the time, perhaps one made in hell.

We exchanged numbers that night to keep in touch. And as I walked back to my hotel room that last night in Laguna beach, he was on the other end of the phone call. I had learned that he had left the band because of some creative differences. So knowing he'd be in the LA area most likely because that's where he was from, I messaged him over Facebook a week or so easier letting him know I'd be down in his area and would love to catch up. We set plans over the phone to hang out the next morning for an early lunch.

As much as Michael and I bonded after that show in Detroit, he was also a bit more new age-y than I was used to at the time. I was still largely within the supposed safety of Christian theology. Michael was someone who grew up, at least to my knowledge, with similar theology but had some beliefs that were a bit far out for me.

As we sat in Laguna Beach eating bowls of organic beans and rice, he talked about the origins of his recognition of, to use my words, Insistence. He talked about being on the boardwalk in Venice Beach. He and former band member, Colin, belted "San Francisco" as the sun cast down on them.

As people walked by.

As the waves crashed beneath them.

He described the memory in such vivid and beautiful detail. The wonder of it seeped out of his mouth and eyes as he visualized the moment.

He talked of the smiles people cast.

And the wonder he felt when he realized this was what humans were capable of.

Love. Communion. Anywhere.

It was a version of heaven he wanted to believe in. And it was here, on this earth, on the Venice Beach Boardwalk of all places.

I let him know how beautiful I thought that memory was. We mused on how, even if all the religions of the world have done their part to add baggage to the realities of the spiritual, moments like his were evidence that there is something beautiful out there that's transcendent.

All around us. Waiting to be discovered.

Michael's words were all the more mind rattling because of

how I had experienced the same thing just a day earlier, during the last day of the conference. Bell had been talking about taking risks and living into the freedom you have tasted from leaving more close-minded spheres behind. Running with the theology of love. A theology that accepts all the good things.

And as he was saying all this, I was in this room with Patrick and Dawn and the stained-glass windows were open and the sun was shining out of them and kids were out for recess at the Montessori school out back and a soft breeze blew in and I knew that this moment, in its collective entirety, was heaven or God and was what I had been chasing.

I knew Michael and I had encountered the same reality even amidst our two different realities. I was beginning to realize the theology of *taste*. Of entering into something, in a risky and vulnerable way, and finding God there. And then discovering through that *entering* that if God's there, he / she / it is probably everywhere else, as long as you give what that something else can be a chance to reveal the Divine Insistence within it.

That's the type of theology I want to give myself to.

At that moment I think I shed the skin of any care I had for anything being seen as too far-out of a belief. Or, to use the term I used earlier, too new age-y.

Because I believe God is everywhere and appearing to everyone.

And encountering God often happens when there's no pretense, and you find yourself in the most unnatural, unassuming, and free of guilt state you can be in.

That doesn't typically happen in the containers of ideology. That happens in the freedom of boardwalks and open-air Montessori school chapel spaces. It's happening in the places where we are free. And freedom without shame is what this conference helped me recognize as being the ultimate pursuit.

The Women (in) God

The whole adventure to Laguna Beach, a trip which was a byproduct of sending an email, was accompanied by another email I got a week before flying southward to the conference.

This email said that I was invited to move into the interview process for the campus ministry role of small group coordinator (SGC) at Whitworth. My bitterness towards all things organized religion had diminished marginally throughout my first fall at Whitworth, and my stance was now in a place of wanting to be, at least cautiously, in such circles again.

The trouble was, the interview time just so happened to be slotted for when I'd be in Laguna Beach learning from Rohr and Bell, the two people who left every religious authority figure at Moody tirelessly frustrated. Queue a bit of liberal theological angst on my part and a naïveté I held that assumed all higher-ed Christians didn't approve of these figures— I replied asking if we could reschedule, because, as I put it rather aloofly, "I have been invited to participate in a conference with Rob Bell and Richard Rohr."

In my mind, this meant no job. However, unbeknownst to me, the woman who received my response was intrigued by a potential thinker outside of the Barthian-inspired theology students she was accustomed to hiring.

. . .

With a fresh tan, salt still lingering in the hair that, at the time, fell beyond my shoulders, and that same hair masking part of my face, I walked into my interview excited about the hypothetical Bible study I, in following the instructions for the interview, had crafted. The study was supposed to focus on the concept of relationships.

"People are turtles in their own ponds," I began.

"And the point is not to force a turtle to leave their pond and head to the others but to have both take canals out of their pond to a pond located in between them. Somewhere in the middle. One where they can both coalesce, yet still find their way back to their own pond if they need to."

The two women interviewing me looked quizzically at each other and looked quizzically at me. I continued.

"It's all about *zimzum*," I said, quoting a concept Bell talked about at the conference.

"We need to create empty space for the other to thrive. That's the definition of *zimzum* and what God did in Genesis when He, if you want to refer to God as a He, that is, separated Himself from creation to allow creation to thrive, but intimately tied Himself to us to make us know what true love is."

"Okay," one of the women said in a long and drawn out way.

My hair had fallen in front of my eyes and partially into my mouth while I talked. I pushed it away, talked about birds for a bit, shook their hands, and walked back to my dorm room.

A week later, much to my surprise, I received an email from my interviewer, Mindy Smith, congratulating me on my new job.

. . .

All of our lives are comprised of a series of colors that fling themselves onto our situation at varying times and in varying stages of our life. These colors are often attributed to the people, experiences, art, etc. that we interact with. The color of deep purple belongs to Mindy. I'm not sure why this is her color, but it is. Maybe the calm but steady and strong boldness it seems to embody? I'm not sure.

It just seems accurate.

There are a lot of things that I have learned about theology through education, rebellion from education, eating bread, my five senses, and fireflies. But in the area of learning what it means to be a Christ-like leader, Mindy doesn't just take the cake; she bakes it. Because she's a leader. And leaders don't just talk about the idea ingredients; they bake them together in action.

Mindy and I started out as boss and worker, and that's what we predominantly were during my junior year, working under her as an SGC.

But when senior year rolled around, we became friends. And along with being a friend, she was my counselor. She helped Emily and I ready ourselves for marriage. She let me come into her office time and time again, sitting on one of two spinning chairs, venting out my soul and my worries and my ideas and my frustrations. And she just sat, as Dave Matthews played in the background, and let me say it all.

She taught me that ideas have to have legs. She taught me that frustration is okay. It's justified. But frustration can never stop you from progressing. Something she was doing during this season herself. She taught me that pushing the limits is okay, but always urged me to analyze the reasoning for pushing the limits.

Quite simply, Mindy gave me one of the truest images of Christ I've ever seen.

And she did this during a time that wasn't always the easiest for her. Because pushing the limits for Mindy simply meant attempting to live into her calling as a woman in ministry, which is something that some people still see as a place only acceptable if tied to Sunday school for children.

Mindy is a wife to Kyle and a mother to Syd and Ash, on top of being a counselor, friend, minister, sense comedic relief, and boss for any and all Whitworth students who seek out the safety of her office. In my experience of leadership within this faith that I, begrudgingly at times, adhere to, Mindy is the one who has undoubtedly shown me what leadership looks like most purely.

. . .

When I was at Moody, there were genuine debates as to whether or not women should be accepted as leaders within the church. People quoted Paul and other verses that seemed to justify one of the more atrocious realities of religious systems, sexism. But it wasn't considered sexism in these circles because it was simply the process of recognizing the "unique abilities" of each sex. Even if such "unique abilities" left women largely on the outside of leadership and liberation, looking in.

And yet, as I've said, the clearest indication of Christ's leadership that I've encountered was in Mindy.

And I've never learned more about the resilience of Christ than I have from looking at my wife Emily and seeing how she loves and cares for people as a nurse so dearly, even with the pain she's gone through. Not to mention she's shown me what it means to push against expectations and not settle for what others expect, but to remain true to who she knows she is.

And I've never experienced a depth of knowledge to theology as I have in my friend Kylie, who studied at Oxford and teaches me some new idea every time we hang out. Kylie was my SGC partner my junior year, without her, I would have been lost. She time and time again taught me more and grew my depth of understanding in theology.

And then there's my mother. Who, from the beginning of my life, has shown me what compromise (if it is warranted) and peacemaking should look like. Not to mention her unending curiosity towards life. She has shown me time and time again that at the end of the day, love always wins.

Anytime there is a theology with a series of don'ts it's likely time to see what it is the don'ts are aligning themselves with.

And my opinion is that the "don't" when it comes to allowing women in ministry is tied to the all too real cowardice of men throughout history who don't like having to keep their arrogance in check. So they use oppression and marginalization as the tool to make it so such things can remain unchecked. Which sounds like a behavior God would be much more against than anything such men might say God is opposed to.

Fear is never a legitimate motivation for a faith based on new life.

To say that women should not preach or be church leaders would very likely have put me, and I'm sure countless others, in a place of hardly knowing Jesus at all.

Laughing at Our Scars

Between my sophomore and junior year of college, my mom had a grandiose idea— to make me see the Midwest as a beautiful place.

It was an attempt to make it have some of the natural allure of the PNW, to prove its aesthetic appeal.

And she did this by taking me to Niagara Falls. Which, for the geographically uninformed, is in the Northeast.

Which, as it turns out, is not the Midwest.

Good try, Mom.

My little sister had befriended a couple of boys from Buffalo, New York, at a summer camp the previous summer. It was a classic broken-hearted young love story of a developing teen. She and a couple of her friends had kept in touch with these Buffalo boys over the course of a year or so, and had planned a reunion.

My mother, in a surprising show of adventure, agreed to be the chauffeur for Catherine and her friends Kenzie and Kalle and asked for me to be her copilot. The trip consisted of a five-to-six-hour drive through the once-thought-of-as-safe country of Canada. Such thoughts were radically changed due to the unexpected actions of a Jeep Grand Cherokee door.

About two-and-a-half-hours into our journey, a combination of a need to rid ourselves of the coffee and tea that had already been consumed, and a need to put more coffee and tea into our systems resulted in a stop off of an Ontario highway.

For those who are unfamiliar, rest stops in Canada, or at least the ones I saw, weren't just toilets and vending machines. These rest stops were like mall food courts, with arcades and gift shops on top of their bathrooms. They were a hub for the northerner on their journey. A place of bustling life amidst miles of rural Ontario farmland.

Our stop was fairly routine. We waited in a long line at Starbucks, my mom bought the Starbucks Canada-themed mug to add to her assortment of Starbucks place-themed mugs, and we made our way back to the car.

At this point, to a twenty-year-old still reveling in the bizarre sleep schedule of a college student, even well into the summer, anything before 11 a.m. was difficult to distinguish between dream and reality. It was around 9:30 in the morning, so such blurriness was still the filter for this experience. As I reached for the car handle on my mother's

Jeep, I swung it open while simultaneously taking a step forward. As if by the uncontrollable actions that are part of dreams, my body seemed to long for injury. And as the door swung one way and my body moved the other way, the two of them reached a point of intersection known as my head.

Me: "Ouch."

Mom: "What happened? OH, MY GOD!"

Me: "What??"

Sister: "Mikey, you're bleeding a lot."

Sister's friends: "Eww, gross."

Me: "Huh? Really? Oh, shoot, HAH. WOW!"

The words were flowing from multiple voices, and what had already been a blur only increased in its way. If at first by sheer confusion from being hit in the head, the blur became physical by the red blur of blood flowing down toward my eyes. My mom left the car to grab ice and napkins. I pulled down the front passenger mirror, only to discover my forehead had lips of sorts, with a mouth open and spewing in a way similar to if it had just been punched in the face.

Also in the reflection of the mirror were the faces of three teenage girls in the backseat in total horror at the blood covered face of the guy in the front seat. It was all rather unsettling. And I was becoming increasingly disoriented. So of course, I got out of the car and headed toward the rural metropolis that was the Canadian rest stop.

Catherine, Kenzie, and Kalle stayed back in the car, my mother was at one of the many counters scrambling to find ice, and I was walking around in a zombie-like fashion between Burger King and Sbarro.

It was likely quite a sight.

Fifteen seconds after the cut happened, my face was covered in blood; now, five or so minutes after the incident, with a flush face and blood dripping onto the floor, I looked like a developing crime scene investigation. And the stares that fell on me seemed to think the same thing.

"Hey. Hey! Buddy, are you okay?" said a voice clearly coming from a well-meaning Canadian, given the nonchalant use of buddy. It was a security guard. With his hand on my shoulder, he took me to a bench and had me sit down. And then I spoke the words no 20-year-old self-described independent would want to say,

"I'm just trying to find my mom."

"We'll find your mom, buddy. Just sit here. Let me get you some ice."

Whether by noticing a stir of commotion or by following the trail of blood that zigzagged around the concourse, it was my mother who, seconds later, found me. After a quick exchange of apologetic thanks to the security guard and with some directions to the local hospital, we made our way back to the car.

I don't really remember what I said on the car ride there; I only remember that a lot of laughing ensued. Which is either a testament to the humor of others in pain or a testament to what my unconscious mind spews out of my mouth. Given my supposed title as a happy drunk, I'll hope for the latter.

Being the young and budding liberal that I was, a part of me wondered if I had pulled this whole stunt purposefully in order to be able to witness universal healthcare in the most personal way possible.

And witness it we did.

When healthcare is free, and when it's summertime in rural Ontario, it seems the social scene is at its pique in a hospital emergency room. There were a good thirty people in there who all seemed to be simply loitering around. Perhaps they were just an audience eager to witness some sort of trauma or looking for a peak to the steady flat line of rural life. Pun intended. Who knows?

But as I walked in with actual blood being part of my emergency, it was as if I was on my last leg. Everyone in the room perked up, the nurses came and got us, and I was ushered to the front of the line.

Upon being led into my room, I was met with one of the most satisfying alignments-with-assumption I've ever had in my life.

Growing up in Michigan and playing hockey for most of my life had made Canadian humor a staple. Saying eh, having a happy-go-lucky drawl, slinging the word buddy around, and using terms like hoser and hosehead were all a part of the early development of my humor. Largely thanks to my Dad introducing me to the faux Canadian comedians Bob and Doug McKenzie at a young age.

As the gauze was removed from my head, the nurse widened her eyes and proceeded to deliver pure Canadian gold—

"Oh, gee whiz! That's quite the cut there ya got on your noodle! How'd ya do that to your noggin?"

Just imagine that previous sentence being spoken from the mouth of Sarah Palin. That's exactly the candor it was spoken in.

Laughing, only to receive a quizzical look back, I explained the situation. The nurse was extremely kind throughout the whole process, cleaned up the cut, and folded the skin back evenly on my head.

"So what do you think I'll need? Just staples for this?" I asked hopefully. At this point in my life I had hair reaching well past my shoulders, and was worried that, with the cut being at my hairline, they'd have to chop some of my hair off. Priorities.

"On no. I don't think so. For this one your gonna need some stitches. The doctor'll be right in ta see ya."

An hour-and-a-half later the doctor walked in.

He was a tall Indian man and informed me that he had a student who was going to help him out with the stitches. He said she'd be adding something like hydrogen peroxide to the cut to get it cleaned out one final time. Then, she'd deliver some shots to my forehead to numb up the stitching spot, and he'd be right back in to stitch it up.

He left. She cleaned. I cringed. She injected. I squirmed. And then proceeded to wait for another fifteen-to-thirty-minutes.

The doctor came back in. As he was prepping his things, we made small talk. He asked me if my injury was the result of a hockey stick coming up high. A wonderful and predictable guess given the country where this hospital bed was located, but not correct.

I swallowed my pride and told him a car door snuck up on me. He laughed and rolled his chair over to peer down at me from above as he readied for his stitching. He pulled the gauze away, and his eyes got huge.

"OH FUCK!"

These were the literal words that came out of the mouth of the doctor who was about to stitch up my head.

"What? What is it?" I asked, concerned.

"Oh, nothing. There's just still a shit ton of blood coming out of here. Can I get more gauze please?"

A nurse came and handed him some. He dabbed my head. I cringed. And the sewing began on the numbed spot atop my noodle.

"All right, you're good to go," they told me after a blurred amount of time.

I walked out to the waiting room where Catherine and friends were watching some Canadian soap opera. It had been over two hours. And yet a fair amount of the same faces who greeted my arrival to the hospital with open-mouthed stares were still sitting around.

Watching TV. Knitting. Rating the stitch work on my forehead.

Only helping me reaffirm my initial assumption that the ER in rural Ontario is a place of incomparable entertainment for the region. Free cable, air-conditioning, and a myriad of injuries. Not to mention, if you did happen to start feeling ill, you could pop on in and have someone feel your noodle for a temperature.

Our journey continued onward. A fresh set of forehead stitches greeted our customs officer as we crossed back into the United States. We had made it to Niagara Falls!

. . .

We all have scars, don't we?

Both physical and metaphorical.

There are things in our past that have happened. Things that have left a permanent mark on who we are.

But isn't it interesting how our understanding of a past scar typically has such a negative connotation? For most of us, myself included, we have been conditioned to believe that scars can only be associated with a memory we'd rather forget.

In the connotation to which they are most regularly associated, scars are a final word for something. They leave no room for renewal.

Now, granted, some things have happened to us and are associated with us that are not currently in a state where renewal is feasible. Yet, at the same time, there are a lot of things that we perceive to be final that are waiting for a new definition.

Scars are like the puppy that pees on you the first time you meet it. Yet, scars are also that same puppy that you adopt and take on prolonged walks fourteen years later as he hobbles along. He looks up at you with the same grin that years earlier meant there was a new yellow stain on the carpet.

Scars are the car you regret spending way too much money on as a single person right after college. Yet it is that same car that you end up taking cross-country with your spouse to move to the place where you're starting your life together.

Scars are the rejection that yields the determination to create a reality far greater than the one that would have resulted from that which you were rejected.

Scars, it would seem, are the negative things waiting to receive a new definition.

I was rather worried to see the amount of blood rushing out of my head in Ontario that summer day. Even if I reflect on it comedically. But in hindsight, I have been able to use that story as a talking point to introduce myself to people. To make people laugh. To help them see me as approachable and relatable.

Because our scars do that. They make us relatable and approachable because everyone has them.

The stories of our scars are a door to connection because everyone has those doors.

I told the friends of my sisters in Buffalo why my forehead was stitched up. They laughed. And then they told me similar stories about themselves. Two teenage, angsty guys who I likely never would have connected with otherwise.

It was my pain tied to their past pain that led to us being able to relate.

That continued to happen with residents in the dorm that I went back to work in a month or so after this happened. I still had the scab from the cut at the time. And I'd tell team members I worked with in the dorm and residents the story.

Emotional scars do this too, in profound ways. Brené Brown, a qualitative research psychologist from Houston, says something to the effect of vulnerability being the springboard to change. When we relay a past pain, we end up finding out that lots of other people have gone through the same thing. And then we relate to them and tell them the funny parts like our head being called a noodle and the painful parts like having shots put into our head.

Scars haunt, and they heal. But they are always there, either way. We just get to decide which trajectory they take.

God Likes to Sing

The summer before my junior year of college, I was home in Michigan, like I was every summer of college. I spent that particular summer working at a summer camp where I took fourth and fifth graders on hikes through a plot of property belonging to a boarding school named Cranbrook. On these hikes, I would point out the croaking of frogs, the buzzing of dragonflies, and the whispering of trees. To which I would receive questions in response like, "when can we eat lunch" or "when can we play soccer" or "why is it so hot?"

It was the summer of the grasshopper. And I don't mean that in some metaphorical sense, even if I was trying to figure out the meaning of why so many of these insects appeared on my body that season. It seemed nearly every day I would have encounters with the bended-knee bug, curiously and fearlessly gazing up into the eyes of a creature (me) one hundred times its size.

The only meaning I could surmise was, like the

grasshopper's leaps did to its journey, this grasshopper was working to propel me into the realization I would later have that summer—that I'm never alone.

And as much as I knew that theoretically, it had to become a truth adopted tangibly, and that tangibility came via the sugar-loving, claw-mouth friend who was always hopping alongside my summer camp instruction, accompanying me seemingly every step of the way.

But the realization also came through the more figurative finding of feeling totally alone and in that aloneness still encountering a presence of something intangible but totally encapsulating. God? Yeah you could call it by that name I suppose. The Great Grasshopper works too.

I digress...

. . .

Early on in high school, I met a couple of kids named Jake and Randy who ushered me into the land of skinny jeans, thrift shop sweaters, and incense.

Jake wore newspaper pants. Randy like patchouli. They were hip.

Over the course of three years together (they were a grade ahead of me) they became really good friends. The connection was made via youth group. A place where, as mentioned previously, I butted heads with a good number of superiors. A butting of heads that, if I'm to be honest, saw more fault on my part than any of there's. I had to rebel against something and this was the place in high school that I could most readily. Our friendship found solace from this place of animosity, however, in a group led by Charlie, who I've mentioned previously.

Charlie, Randy, Jake, Jimmy, and I, along with a few other guys, would gather once a week, play soccer, talk about God, and then go home. It was a setup not all that unlike other youth groups.

But then senior year rolled around, Jimmy didn't want to go anymore, Randy and Jake went off to college, and Charlie had an existential crisis.

And so the group disbanded.

The summer of the grasshopper also happened to be the summer Randy got married. As I drove up to the venue on the day of his wedding, I looked out the window at the rearview mirror on the outside of the car, and, because this was just the way the summer was, saw a pale green grasshopper looking back at me.

As I drove on Adams Road in the deciduous Oakland county of southeast Michigan, I had a hard time looking in front of me because of what sat on top of the device that allowed me to see behind. The grasshopper, in either heroic fashion or stubbornness, was still clinging to the mirror thirty minutes into the drive.

I pulled into the dirt driveway of the wedding venue, found a spot a little way away, got out of the car, and cupped my hands around the little bug still on the mirror. There were trees and tall grass on the north side of the lot. So I, with hands creating a cavern, slowly walked over to the green edge of the lot.

I set him on the grass, said a few parting words, and made my way over to the venue where I met Jake. His pants weren't newspaper lined anymore. And although he had chosen to move out to Spokane himself a year earlier and cause consistent confusion about which Jake friend I was referring to, this was the first I had seen him in months.

The whole event was beautiful. Modesty mixed with a spark of formality. It all made perfect sense for a wedding between Randy and his long time girlfriend Riann.

But it was also an incredibly peculiar setting because of the reality of *time*. At the table where I sat, there was Claudia, one of my best friends in high school and my long-thought romantic destiny (like that phrasing? Yikes.) She was with her boyfriend, Samir. And then there was Jake, Mike, and Charlie and his girlfriend. It was like everything from the past had accelerated three years without existing in the time in-between. I was a part of the moment, but was only part of it because of a past I had moved away from, literally and emotionally.

This feeling only heightened when I later left the dance floor and sat back down in my seat to observe the sweaty chaos I had just come from. There were so many people I cared about packed onto that slab of hardwood floor. I was incredibly close to love, looking at it from my seat, but also distant from it. And, as my mind peered into the meta, the bigger picture of things, I realized that was exactly how I felt about the relationships I held with the people dancing. Close to the love I had for them, but distant. Literally, because of moving away after high school, and figuratively with the state of emotion tied to those dynamics and how they had grown less prevalent in my life with the passing of time.

I suddenly felt very alone.

This was the same feeling my departure from the faith of my childhood for a newer more open faith had left me with. I was close to something because I could theorize about it. I had read about this new thing, talked about it, and wrote about it. But it wasn't a faith I felt I was able to dance with yet.

"Mikey, I got a ride home with Alex's sister. You don't have to worry about dropping me off anymore," Jake said interrupting my introspection.

I was free to drive back alone. Earlier that night I had seen on Twitter, in one of the impulsive refreshes I'm all too guilty of, that my favorite band at the time, Night Beds, had released a single off of their upcoming album. Not having Jake in the car gave me the perfect outlet to listen to it bombastically; letting whatever emotion it yielded pour out.

Night Beds had been my band of the summer. The band was a project of a guy named Winston Yellen. Whatever had been the source of his melodramatic lyrics also had spoken to me. His album *Country Sleep* seemed to tell the story of a young man struggling with getting in the way of himself but longing for hope all the same. It was deeply spiritual for me. And absurdly relatable. As I mentioned, I was still trying to figure out what it meant to live authentically, a process that had began with the stark pain that being rejected by Emily had initially caused in me.

A state of melancholy such as the one I was having in my chair outside the dance floor paired nicely with the melancholic desperation in Yellen's pleading calls for a new start that *Country Sleep* yielded. It was an album recognizing little beauties, yet still mourning the beauty that was unattainable. Sort of like the presence of a grasshopper on the way to a wedding of a friendship existing mostly in the past.

So, as I loaded into the car, I queued the new song. It was called "Finished" and would be the opening track to the new album Night Beds was putting out the following week. And it was music like I can't remember ever hearing. It was one part classical, one part electronic, one part folk, all parts ethereal. And as the moon hung to my left out the window, full and alive, I felt the type of emotion that is slow to come over you. As if it is the tide slowly working its way inward. Slowly at first but increasing steadily to a point where you feel surrounded by it. And, before you know it, you're totally submerged.

After the song was over, I put on Night Beds' first album. I hit the shuffle button, and a song I swore I never remember having ever heard came on. I had listened to this album all summer, and it was like I was listening to this particular song for the first time. The song played as I drove down the tree canopy covered Adams Road in Bloomfield Hills, Michigan. The song told the story of the narrator not wanting to be alone anymore, that he had done this to himself, isolating his true self from reality. Putting up a false front.

It was something my hyperemotional mind identified with.

And then the narrator of the song moved into asking an unknown character of the scene, which I interpreted to be God, if this figure cared at all. It had watched him cause all this pain. Seen him angry with himself. And seemingly never intervened. The song, titled Lost Springs, allowed the God character to respond but only after the frustration had been fully verbalized by the narrator. And all the response kept urging was that, he, she, it would never leave and had never left the narrator on their own. That the narrator didn't have to worry anymore. That they could live into the reality of the world freely.

I wept as the song played. I heard this as a conversation between God and me. I knew I was living a false front, trying to get all my ideas and concepts and thoughts so perfectly formulated and organized that it was inhibiting my ability to see the beauty attached to the gift of life. God seemed to be telling me that I'd never be on my own. And I realized that this reality would only truly be felt when I gave myself over to living life as opposed to theorizing about it. It would be then that I'd truly start tasting the goodness that was tied to life.

I began to see that a grasshopper on my ankle could be a gift, simply. And it didn't have to be theorized about, but just accepted for the beauty and subtlety it that it spoke to. A beauty and subtlety that I now believe is all around us. Not waiting to be interpreted, but encountered.

A Portland Pilgrimage

I was moping about in October, as is my tradition during that month, when I learned that Night Beds was having a concert dedicated to playing the entirety of their album *Country Sleep.* The album I listened to endlessly that summer of self-realization or self-actualization or coming-of-age, whatever you want to call it. And I also learned that it would be in Portland. Only about a six-hour drive from Spokane.

It was a no-brainer. I was going.

I borrowed a car from someone I knew at church and split some gas with a buddy named Joseph who lived outside of Portland and was going to let me crash at his family's place.

I overdramatized the whole deal. Because that is my tendency.

I told my friends I was going on a pilgrimage. A transition from a stage of thought to one of living. Seeking out the things I had theorized about. In hindsight, it is all a bit comical. But it is the crafting of narrative that turns any collection of moments into a story. And I think there's importance to that.

I dropped Joseph off at his house and drove to some obscure restaurant to meet a social media friend. Social media friends are a quintessential millennial reality. I had come in contact with a girl by the name of Alex via our mutual love for Night Beds. It was strictly platonic. She was involved in a serious relationship, and I was in the midst of reconnecting with Emily, so we were able to meet up and simply talk about the power of music without the awkward tension of hormones. We did this over dinner, talking about the songs that have spoken to us the most. I told her about my experience with "Lost Springs." She told me about "The Book of Love" by The Magnetic Fields. We tracked with each other. Real music lovers with the same music taste. Two people who tied music and life into a commentary we wrote in our minds, with every lyric we took the time to listen to making up its prose.

The venue for the show was an old Baptist church downtown. However, even with this being the venue, there was no reason to believe Yellen, the singer, was a Christian. His music dealt with young adult angst. Drug and alcohol-inspired highs and lows. Love and loss.

There were some commentaries on God in his music, but the way I had interpreted most of them were often a result of my reading into the lyrics to find what I was searching for, like I did with *Lost Springs*. It was me following the whole *what you seek, you will find* philosophy.

This trip I happened to be seeking divine intervention. And the last place I expected to find that, in my cynical religious state at that point in my life, was a church. Especially a Baptist one. But that's where the show was happening.

Right before going in, there was a flock of birds all flowing collectively up and down with a backdrop of gray autumn northwest sky. The birds seemed to all come together, from all their differing tree branches and nests, for this one moment of collective experience.

Like all of us filtering into the venue.

Like all of my assumptions and expectations coming into this weekend.

"You ready for this," Alex whispered as we filtered in with the rest of the crowd.

I was. I nodded. Music is so special. So, so special.

It's such a remarkable shaper of identity. Even if we don't have the experience singers have when they write the songs they write, we pick certain songs to be our anthems. I was going to hear the album anthem of my life in its entirety live, and the song that set me on track to be at peace with life and love and to slow down my thought process on such things and instead start living.

I understand how that can sound silly and dramatic. But anyone who's had a song or a band or an album speak to them likely knows where I'm coming from.

142

What ensued was as bizarre as I should have expected, due to the unfair amount of meaning I was giving to this pilgrimage weekend. The opening act came up, and he began belting worship songs. Songs I would've expected to hear at church. Which, to be fair, was where I was as I sat in a pew. But it was so unexpected for a show that featured a headlining artist who sang about such wide-ranging topics.

I listened to these songs without the predictable cynicism of my past, but as songs truly trying to express gratitude to something bigger than us. And I was moved. To tears, actually. In this moment I saw worship not as cheap like I had for so long, but as an expression, like all music, to a reality bigger than just the singer and listener.

Yellen of Night Beds came on. He was playing solo. His voice carried into every square inch of the heightened ceilings and soared into each one of my emotional corners as well. It was powerful. And chilling.

Lost Springs is towards the end of the album. But everything leading up to it created a heightened sense of excitement because of just how powerful the simple combination of voice, guitar and high ceilings were.

All I had found out about the song was that *Lost Springs* is the name of a town in Wyoming. But the town isn't much of a town at all really.

It has a population of one.

The first thing this pointed to was the reality of isolation as a theme in the song, which was something I had felt the past summer. And that isolation leads to desperate pleas for purpose, connection, and true meaning. Hence the conversing at the end of the song about never wanting to be on one's own, and the rebuttal saying that the narrator would never be left on their own. But the other recurring lyric in the song, was the question of,

Oh, are you able? Oh, are you faithful?

Meaning, at least to me, will you choose to align with such connection?

Yellen began playing the song. Alex nudged me; she knew it was my moment. I closed my eyes and just breathed in every sound wave I could. I was covered in a blanket of shivers. I felt like I was floating throughout the whole song.

I was taken back to the moment on Adams Road when I first had heard it and thought about the few months since then in which I had started to live into the reality of life with purpose as opposed to living life through the lens of ideas. It was all very serious for a largely intangible thing, yes, but I was having a moment.

And I knew it was big, whatever it was. The song ended— but it didn't end. There wasn't fingerpicking on any of the live or recorded versions that I had ever heard, but that's what followed what would have usually been the conclusion. And then one final refrain, with new lyrics to the song, which I also hadn't seen on any videos or heard on any recordings.

Lord, you are able. Lord, you are faithful.

When these words were spoken, I recognized the mirrored reality of singer and listener and God literally being something all around and connecting things in mysterious and confusing and bewildering ways. This song was about the exact experience or state of emotion I was in when I had heard it. That I/we are never on our own when tied to something bigger. It was such an elementary spiritual thought, but it hit me so hard I couldn't shut up about it for a year.

But there's the question of why. Why did this speak to me so much? Because you probably read this passage and thought it was cool, maybe a bit beautiful, but not the most profound thing you've ever read.

And yet, that's exactly how I encountered it. As paradigm shifting. As monumental. I still don't know exactly why. But my best guess is that an idea had aligned itself with reality. And what I had realized when I first heard the song was that all of my theories about God and life and living weren't helping me actually experience the world. The purpose the writer wrote it for seemed to align with the very idea needed to be spoken to me back then.

I put a lot of stake in my reality being tied to the reality of the person who wrote the song. And the words "Lord, you are able, Lord, you are faithful" satisfied that stake. We like it when our reality aligns with another reality, at least I do. It evokes a certain recognition of oneness. A reality that we are in this together. That it's all okay.

And when there's a bridge from our experience to another

person's experience, we feel justified in the experience. Because wherever two or more experiences reside, there can be truth and transformation. Isolation has no accountability. We need to be united to feel connected. Which is obvious. And this song that spoke so much to me had a meaning that its very crafter and I were united in. Coming back to a place of peace via trust. And when you can be united in experience with the creator of that experience, it can be a profound reality.

Frozen Chameleons

The next day I went back to Portland. I was high on a sense of mystical divine intercession, the actuality of an experience I had hoped or theorized God was made up of. A fluid and free firefly rather than the captured one of doctrine. I had encountered the reality of the Divine without the pretext of how or where. And as I skipped along in the hipster town of bridges and coffee, someone entered into my glee, saying, "Sure is a beautiful day, isn't it?"

I turned to my right. A homeless man was seated on a concrete slab next to Starbucks. His statement seemed to come as a by-product of him simply witnessing my existence; it certainly not a reflection of the cloudy Portland weather hovering above us.

I replied, "Yeah, yeah it is! Big time. What's your name?"

This exchange opened the gate to a door wanting to be made ajar. The man's name was Aaron. He wanted a

Frappuccino, and, as would become clear an hour later, as we would still be chatting, he also wanted someone to talk to.

If the day before I had encountered a bit of my heaven on earth, hearing Aarons story was a bit like discovering hell.

He told me about how he had lived on the East Coast. And how everything had been good for the most part. He was in love with a woman, and they had a good life together. No kids yet, but they wanted to settle down. They dabbled with heavy drugs every now and again, but they were always right on the brink of being done, "This is the last time," he said, quoting himself talking to his love with a painfully regret ridden tone.

But on one of the numerous "last times," something went wrong. Aaron was strung out on heroin, as was his girlfriend. But this time things didn't go as they normally had. She started coughing, choking, gagging, shaking—and then was still. Aaron, paralyzed from his own high, watched as the woman he loved choked on her vomit.

As he told me this, his eyes darted to-and-fro, saying over and over that *they* were watching. Pointing to one person and then another as people walked by on the street. He appeared schizophrenic, paranoid by something. He continued his story.

The family of his girlfriend came knocking the next day. They knew what the two of them were up to. They were trying to get her to check in every night to make sure she was not using drugs anymore. Aaron fled with his pet chameleon. He didn't know what else to do. His voice became more frantic, troubled, deeply, by the recollection of his past. This fleeing led him to find work at a farm. He worked in the fields and was invited to stay in the compound-like house. One night, when he came back from the field, his chameleon was missing. He couldn't find it anywhere until it turned up in the freezer of the landowner he described as, "deeply disturbed." The chameleon was dead with wounds on its body.

He bummed his way out west. And now, in his delusional state, he saw the henchmen of the landowner who killed his chameleon in the groups of people that passed by on the Portland sidewalks. He doesn't know where to go. He just needs something like the simple joy of the sugar in a Frappuccino.

My high-on-life state took a drastic dive bomb upon hearing all of this. I didn't know what to believe, or if I should alert someone. But he also talked to me about love. And we spoke about the mystery of the beautiful things in life, and how we both believed love trumped the pain of the world. But when I left him, it seemed like that wasn't true. I sensed the darkness of his hauntings following me. I looked at people differently. The world seemed to have a darker filter. I was alarmed. I drove back to Joseph's place and couldn't shake that feeling until after we got back to Spokane.

The weekend in Portland saw a rise and fall, beauty and pain. And I've been reminded ever sense that any beautiful reality must also be held alongside the painful ones. And that ultimately the most beautiful realities aren't the ones of independent beauty, but the ones that give pain a new trajectory. That give what is stagnant and stuck new vitality and energy. And I don't think it's any coincidence that on a trip that helped keep propelling myself forward, I spent a good long while talking to someone who was stuck. There's a tension to life.

Some people are free flowing and evolving and growing. But others can't move, they are frozen like the chameleons of their past, stuck in a shade of regret and pain. And it's not the fault of the individual. But the more we walk in tandem, the more the trajectory of something collective can progress, become un-stuck, and see a new day.

. . .

I was counting out loud in the car the other day when I suddenly stopped and used the open-ended word of wonder,

"Whoa."

"What's up?" Emily asked.

"Can you technically have like zero point one billion?"

"Yeah, that's a thing," Emily said, laughing at my curiosity.

"So, there's infinity between every number, just as there's infinity with numbers themselves? So, if you were to count all the possibilities between zero and one you could never even really count to one?"

"Yeah! That's an idea that John Greene talks about in that

book that was really popular, *A Fault in Our Stars*."

I was a bit discouraged that my realization was a theme in a hugely popular book for young adults. But I set my ego aside. What I had just become aware of is an idea largely talked about in computing circles and, apparently, teen romantic fiction.

If you truly and holistically try to count from one to two, you won't be able to do it. It would take an infinite amount of time because of the infinite amount of numbers that are between the numbers one and two.

Which is a lot like each of our stories.

We have a propensity to see someone as *just* _____ when that someone is, supposedly, lower in the social circles we are typically comfortable in. This happens in all cultures and all spheres. Certain people are ascribed to certain levels of status, which are supposedly a gauge of their worth.

Aaron is *just* a homeless person to a lot of people.

But what if we are to think of people as numbers?

What if - within every single human being in the world - there is an infinite amount of complexity, and by glossing over those people just like we gloss over the full scope of the number one when we immediately jump to the number two, we miss out on a certain level of depth?

I believe depth to be intimately tied to wonder. I think they coalesce in the same neighborhood. Actually, more specifically, I believe that it is in recognizing the depth of things that we can recognize the wonder in them.

To me, numbers never held very much wonder. They were just tools. But when you think about the infinity between each, they become fascinating!

When we limit someone to simply a title or create a hierarchy where some are simply defined by being *beneath* or *just,* we miss the possibility to see the infinity that is tied to their them-ness. Because if numbers can have an infinite amount of depth and nuances and possibility, people certainly can too.

Spider Webs

During the summer after I graduated from college, I read an essay where Mary Oliver reflects on a spider and its web that she happened to notice while she was renting a home for a season. She talked about the spider and its web in a way only Mary Oliver can talk about such things. Her language was of such wonder, beauty, and observance that I as a reader couldn't help but feel I was slowly being pulled into the spider web myself. Not to become trapped in a merciless way, but more in a soft and restful way. The web Mary Oliver was painting brought peace.

When I worked at the Young Authors Day Camp in Michigan, there were a couple of days that one of my parents would have to drop me off early because of the musical chairs my family played with our cars. During these early mornings, I would do what I didn't have the freedom to do during the day, and that was wander around the wooded acres of Cranbrook with only the noise of the natural environment and my footsteps.

The best word to describe the setting was serene. I felt alone, but overwhelmingly welcome. Which is a feeling I'm convinced only nature knows how to yield. The sun would always be casting itself. Do you know what I mean? Like when the light from it is not so much an illuminator, but more like a beam. Breaking steadily through the leaves above and placing its spotlight on the dancing dust of the air. Turning gnats and dirt into fairies for the imagination.

There was one morning in particular when I was making my way through the woods, and the spotlight of cast sunlight illuminated a spiderweb in the middle of the path. And it did so in a way so serenely that it could only be explained as the result of something intended. The rays of the sun, millions upon millions of miles away, found themselves seated here. In this three-foot-by-three-foot web. In southeastern Michigan. And the web and the oh-so-distant light were cooperating in the same way as a light master and actor. Partners in the pursuit of wonder.

Amidst the spotlight, there was a spider. Sitting about six or so inches from a fly that it had caught. Prideful, likely. Patient, certainly. The spider didn't jump right on its morning meal but seemed to be waiting instead for brunch. Gazing past the gruesome reality of reality, I saw the outer edges of the web. One edge was attached to a tree branch above and slightly to the right. Another edge was attached to a leaf on the opposite side of the path, lower and to the left. The web, in all its glory, was outstretched in four or five different spots, reaching to different plants which were disconnected outside of the construct of the web itself.

It was all quite wonderful to take in. I sat there observing it all for a good three minutes before I carefully ducked myself below the web, and continued on my walk, not daring to take the kiddos past these parts. Nothing that connects so many independent things in oneness should be corrupted. And that's what a steady line of humans likely would have done, unintentionally or intentionally.

. . .

The other day I was talking to Emily about love and God and how we know that Divine love exists. I don't know if you can know. I think that may be an arrow pointing towards the wrong mark.

I see God as love. Nothing less. And there is nothing more. So, to separate God from love is a bit like separating breath from life. It doesn't work.

And then I began to think about love and what it is and how we can clue into divinity because of love etc. And then I thought of the spider web.

As we drove to Branches, our church, for an event, I had a vision of love that was a bit like the web at Cranbrook. The web was connecting multiple aspects of the landscapes. Things seemingly unconnected until the spider found a way to tie them all together to capture nourishment for its life. And as I looked at all the people driving around us, I began to think about how different they all were, but how they all loved someone and someone loved them.

"You know what's cool," I said, without letting Emily ask what.

"Every single person we're driving by right now, all of them, they all love someone. And someone loves them. Think about that! Imagine that everyone has strands of a web springing off of them that extend to all the different people they love. Now imagine that every human being that has ever existed and is existing has those strands exiting and entering them."

"Keep going," Emily said.

"If this were the case, we wouldn't be able to move. We'd be trapped. We'd be like a fly in a web. But we wouldn't be trapped in something leading to our doom. We'd be trapped in the hope that allows us to keep going. We'd be trapped in the overwhelming amount of love that exists in the world. I think God is that web. And that comforts me."

. . .

There are a lot of days that can be hard. And we can feel like the ability to keep going is as distant as the light of the sun in the dark days of winter. But there is always love around you. Even if you don't feel it, even if you don't see it, it's there. And if it were as objective as the webs of a spider, it would be so abundant and in-your-face that you wouldn't even be able to move. Because you'd always be locked in its grasp. And what a great grasp to be caught in! The strands of love are always waiting to catch you.

Junior Year

Junior year at Whitworth saw a number of new dynamics filter into my life. For the first time, I was leaving Michigan to be greeted by a family member out west. Jack, my older brother, had been doing a summer internship at a golf course in Coeur d'Alene, Idaho which is only about thirty minutes east of Spokane.

Jack and I spent a good amount of time together on weekends when he wasn't working, which meant that I spent a good amount of time away from my work. I was in the early phases of coordinating small groups for a residence hall on campus. My partner in this job, Kylie, had a certain affinity for structure. Something I don't share. In the slightest.

And then there was also the reconnection with Emily. Since our last go, or my last attempt at pursuit, Emily had dated someone else. They had been together for almost half a year but had split towards the end of the summer. Which, selfishly, left me at least the tiniest bit satisfied. We had chatted via text only once over the summer, but both of us had expressed that it would be fun to catch up. We went to a farmers' market in the first month of junior year. I bought her a pumpkin. We were hanging out as *just friends* who were both in personal rebuilding phases, and we found mutuality in that rebuilding. Emily had gone through a tough breakup. I was trying to redefine myself by reality as opposed to philosophical theory. We bonded over the process of self-reconstruction throughout the fall. When you care for someone for who they are, not who you need or want them to be, you'd be amazed by what can happen.

. . .

The most humorous dynamic of the year was the one I shared with the person who slept about five feet from me that year, my roommate Brad. Some people are your best friend. Some people are a pain in the ass. Brad was something else—undefinable.

The dynamic of having a college roommate is really quite a fascinating thing. As an eighteen-year-old, you start your life at a brand-new place that you are likely completely unfamiliar with. And right when you start that process, you are placed in a room with another person who you likely have never met in your life. And you are asked to get along with this person, sleep within feet of this person, and accommodate the idiosyncrasies of this person for a full year. The only other place this type of thing happens is in prison cells.

Roommates and college were not the two most complimentary words for me between the ages of eighteen and twenty-one. My first roommate, Jake, was one of my groomsmen, years later. We went to Moody together, and are still good friends. We make each other laugh uncontrollably. But he was a horrible roommate because of one simple, but obsessive, flaw—CrossFit. Jake is more of a lab tube human than a college guy. He woke up every morning at 4:30 a.m. to the same song, which went with his whole CrossFit routine. And I'd wake up with him. Unwillingly. And be reminded of the fact that my body would remain stationary in bed while Jake's heart rate would spike to a place of vitality and his muscles would expand.

Sophomore year there was Mo. Mo stacked all of our furniture in the middle of the room and left a bunch of condoms on top of it. I encountered this work of modern art before I even met Mo, as I walked into the dorm room to drop of my things. Like I already mentioned, Mo had an affinity for some heavy drugs and a room scented by weed. And he snored. Louder than anyone I've ever met. And played League of Legends until 3 a.m.

But Brad. Brad was a whole new dynamic. I was a junior living on campus because of my job coordinating residence hall small groups. My roommate for that year was slotted to be my best friend at Whitworth at the time, Alex. The year was gearing up to be one of endless NHL on the Xbox and laid-back conversation, a familiar dynamic. But Alex transferred at the last minute to play baseball at a different school.

. . .

I had taken it upon myself to bunk our beds before Brad got there. I figured my seniority as a junior warranted such things. But it only took one night to realize that was a mistake.

Poor Brad was the classic case of trepid freshman. He was tall and very skinny. His body moved a little bit like those balloon people in front of car dealerships. And he had a certain fondness for the words "I'm sorry," the use of which could have been easily avoided by quick use of the tool known as common sense.

The first night Brad and I shared a room was a bit of a foreshadowing for the confusion of the rest of the year. I had fallen asleep or was on the verge of such things when Brad walked in. I heard him climbing in a stealthy way up to the top bunk. Upon reaching his destination, there was a bang on the wall beside my head. His phone had fallen from the top bunk, between the bed and the wall. I heard him jump down from the top bunk. And then it happened. I still sleep under my covers as a grown man, so the next course of Brad movements was largely reliant on my sense of touch. I suddenly felt the blankets above me being pressed down. And then the soft whisper of "Oh my God, oh my God, I'm sorry, I'm so sorry." Brad was leaning over the top of my body, looking for his phone. Had I been asleep, his whispering would have been a surefire way to break that state.

"Brad, what are you doing?"

"Uh, I'm sorry..."

And up Brad went to the top bunk without another word.

At 5:30 a.m., the most obnoxious noise erupted beside my ear. The noise was an alarm coming from a phone, and that phone certainly wasn't mine at such an outrageous hour. I heard a thud on the floor next to me. I was still under the covers but knew such a loud thudding could only be the result of a six-foot-three-inch freshman falling from his bed. "Oh my God, oh my God, I'm sorry, I'm so sorry," Brad repeated once again as he pressed his body over the top of mine, looking for his phone, which he found. And then he climbed back up into bed.

. . .

More events followed throughout the year. Brad would always turn the lights on when he walked into our room at night. I politely asked him to stop as I was sleeping when this would happen. He politely agreed. Our first night after the conversation, I was again close to sleep. The door opened. Brad walked in and turned on the light. I figured I'd give him a couple of minutes or so. After those minutes passed and the light was still on, I flipped my body over toward his desk, as I had been facing the wall. As I flipped, our eyes locked. He was sitting in a chair no more than three feet from me, with a sketchbook in his lap and pencil in his hand. My imagination was mortified. He shot up without allowing me to say a word, ran to the light, saying, "Oh my God, I'm so sorry," over and over, shut the light off, and left the room.

There was another occurrence where he disappeared. I hadn't seen him in a couple of days. My resident assistant and I were getting concerned. He wasn't answering his phone. And then I got a Facebook message from his parents asking if I knew where he was because they couldn't get a hold of him. I said no. We all pooled our resources to find him. A day later, I got a message from him saying he was sorry, but his phone died. He had, acting on a sudden impulse, driven fifteen hours to attend a conference.

Brad did odd things. But despite his odd tendencies, Brad had a good heart and gave a certain level of comedic lightness to a busy beginning to the year. A year that would be beautiful and fresh, but also one that would reveal tangible pain in the life of someone I care about.

San Francisco and Loss

My brother Jack and I's biggest road trip endeavor was one we took over my fall break to San Francisco. The trip fell right after my twenty-first birthday. My best friend as a kid, Jimmy, was going to fly into Spokane to join us. And our cousin Chris had a flight into San Jose, saving room in the car for the bulk of the drive. From San Francisco, I'd fly back to Spokane, Jack would drive back home to Michigan, as his internship had ended, and Chris and Jimmy would fly back to Detroit.

There are certain things, like salt and caramel and chicken and waffles, that you don't think will mesh well when advertised together. But they do, in a weird way. And you don't really question it; you just keep on eating. Which was a bit like the dynamic tied to the four of us as we walked around Chinatown in San Francisco, drove the 101 through Big Sur, and stared at jellyfish at the Monterey Bay Aquarium.

Chris is a mini-Jerry Seinfeld, having his laugh and constant comedic relief was definitely a highlight. Jimmy is a complainer. Not necessarily in a serious way, more in a gripe-to-start-conversation kind of way. He's quick to roll his eyes. I'm always overanalyzing and trying to read into things. And Jack is very task driven and wants everything to have a tangible purpose. Humor, attitude, overanalysis, and intention are all good qualities in certain respects but form an odd stew. I think everyone encountered the trip in their own way, which is the fascinating part.

Jimmy has been my friend longer than anyone who is not blood-related to me. We met around the time of first grade, when Jack and Jimmy's sister, Colleen, played on the same hockey team. We'd make up weird activities to do around the perimeter of the rink during their games. As we grew older, we'd spend nearly every day together in the summers. We went through all sorts of phases. One phase of playing nothing but Tiger Woods PGA Tour 2005. Jimmy could never get a hole in one. I once got one having one hand on the controller, while on the phone. Another phase was when Jimmy's mom let us know she had a bunch of frozen hamburgers in the basement that would go bad in a month, so we had to start eating them. So, as eighth graders, we made our own specialty burgers once a day for a good two weeks. We, along with the third of the three amigos, Noah, built a wooden go-kart that Jimmy broke twice before Noah or I even had the chance to ride it. We made random YouTube videos. We went to concerts together. Jimmy, even with all his feisty-attitude tendencies, was my best friend growing up.

But an aspect of Jimmy's life that never really was discussed was his dad. My earliest memories of going over to his house all had his dad in roughly the same place, a chair where he'd watch cycles of Detroit Red Wings games, responding to whatever happened on the screen with a sense of ornery frustration. My parents let me know pretty early on that he had Alzheimer's, which I couldn't comprehend the meaning of at all when I was first told it. But I recognized it as a bit of detachment from the setting he was in.

Jimmy and I would never really talk about this part of his life. His mom would occasionally bring it up when I was over, more so as we got older, to which Jimmy would become visibly annoyed and want to talk about something else. I think I recall bringing it up once or twice between the years of the third and twelfth grade. But not often. Because as an adolescent guy, you're not taught to relay feelings, which is one of the more troubling dynamics of how our culture operates. We are taught to keep things down because the emotional isn't for display. I'm not Jimmy, so I don't know how he wrestled with it; I still don't really. And it isn't my business to assume. Because it is his story. But there was an instance on this trip to California where the avoidance impacted my story, and I still think of it an astounding amount.

I want to say that it was our second to last day of the trip, the last full day, that is. Jimmy, Chris, and I were taking our respective flights the next afternoon to our two different locations. Them to Detroit, me to Spokane. We were in Carmel. It's a small town sandwiched between Monterey and the northern tip of Big Sur. The setting was unbelievably surreal. The four of us were standing on the shores of the Pacific Ocean. I was taking slow-motion videos of the waves. Jimmy was throwing stuff into the water. Jack and Chris were facing the other direction looking up at Pebble Beach, the world-renowned golf course that jutted up to the sand we stood on. And that's when nature hit. Jimmy and I both had to go the bathroom.

So, we wandered up the beach to the stone beach bathroom. And as I was still in my stall and Jimmy was washing his hands, his phone rang. He walked out and answered it at the same time. I took a few more minutes thanks to coffee, but then walked out and saw him a little ways off, still on the phone. I minded my own business and looked at one of the unique trees near the shore. Jimmy hung up about thirty seconds later and wandered over.

"Everything all good?" I asked.

"Yeah. Yeah, it's fine," Jimmy said.

As we walked back toward the water, rather silently, Jack and Chris were walking back up our direction.

"Chris and I were thinking we should do the 17-Mile Drive. It costs a little, but we can all throw in," Jack said as we met them. The 17-Mile Drive is exactly what it says it is, a drive that is seventeen miles. But it follows an unimaginably beautiful stretch of coast and goes out to a place known as Spanish Bay and to the famous Lone Cypress.

As we drove, three elements of our four-part dynamic

played out. Jack was meeting an agenda requirement, Chris cracked some joke about the four of us spending time in a specialty soap shop earlier, and I tried to figure out some metaphor tied to the waves and rocks. But Jimmy, instead of making some wisecrack at these metaphorical attempts, was mostly silent.

When we got to the Lone Cypress, we all piled out of the car to take pictures and get a good look at the world's most photographed tree. This cypress sits out on a jetty of rock in the Pacific Ocean. It's completely isolated from the rest of its kind. Still part of the land and the forest near it, but out in the sea. At the mercy of the gray crashing of the Pacific. Jack and Chris had wandered to some other part of the trail while Jimmy and I remained on the wooden deck that overlooked the tree. I was in an artsy photo phase at this point in my life and snapped one of Jimmy. He was alone at the railing, the cypress over his shoulder, past the tree the horizon was all water. The sky was covered in gray clouds. You could make out tiny little cells miles out in the water that poured rain out of them. It was just a lone Jimmy, a lone cypress, and thousands upon thousands of miles of water. I couldn't help but wonder what he was thinking. My mind immediately jumped to his brother, Tommy, who was thousands of miles across that water in South Korea teaching English. And how maybe Jimmy was thinking about him. Or maybe it had something to do with the phone call? Or maybe I was making all these possibilities up because of my mind of overanalysis, and his hunched-over figure was simply tied to the reality that Jimmy felt carsick, and the ocean background that looked like the infinite unknown was simply just the reality of our location. I couldn't really know. And Jimmy is not the type who would take to conversing about such thoughts, clueing me in on which one held the truth. I'd have to wait for my phone to buzz later at dinner to know the answer to that.

We ended up eating dinner at some pub at Spanish Bay with a guy Jack knew who worked there. In between bites of a bacon cheeseburger, my phone vibrated.

"How's Jimmy doing?" read the text from my Mom.

"I looked over at him. He hadn't eaten much and was quiet. But that was pretty standard Jimmy behavior when around people that he didn't know super well, like Chris and Jack.

"Seems fine. I think he's been having a good time. Why do you ask?" I replied.

"He hasn't told you? His mom just called me. His dad passed away this afternoon."

There's a certain type of frozen that happens in moments where the level of emotion is far beyond your control, your grasp, or your understanding. And that's the frozen I suddenly felt. I ached in such a hard way for Jimmy. I wanted to tell him I was there for him. But my interpretation of his silence was his lack of desire to disclose. I was someone who loved seeking meaning. Loved to dive into the deep conversations of things. Loved to weigh the emotion. Jimmy was not like this, not in the slightest. And this was his reality, his pain, not mine. And I felt this bizarre feeling that happens when you have to care for someone how they want to be cared for, not how you think they should be cared for. Also known as... truly caring for someone.

I approached Jimmy about it the next morning as we walked to find an ATM. I told him I was there for him if he ever wanted to chat about it. He thanked me but largely pushed it aside. I still think of that picture I took of him. A picture of grief or pain or unknown or whatever it was he was feeling, all bottled up.

I spend a lot of my time wanting to talk about things. Wanting to go deep with people. But I've also spent nearly all of my time alive riding a pretty steady wave, not having to face a lot of loss or pain. The longing to dive deep without having encountered the realities of the deepness of pain itself was a reminder that reality is far more complex and dynamic than theory. Which is, or should be, obvious.

Just as the four of us who drove around on that trip in Jack's little Chevy Cruze had drastically differing personalities, the way people interact with the realities of hardship and pain differ too. And time and time again I've tried to get myself to learn the importance of putting the human encountering the reality before the ideology I have for dealing with the reality. But that's incredibly hard. Radically difficult. Because we humans want to fix things. We don't like there being brokenness in life.

. . .

The Japanese have this old practice that is a part of their pottery making. It's a practice directly dealing with the unplanned. It's called *Kintsugi*. The idea is that when a piece of pottery shatters, you should attempt to mend it by not trying to hide the cracks but highlighting them with a golden, silver, or copper lacquer. The cracks of the broken piece of pottery are highlighted, exposed, and on display.

But if someone were to see a potter drop their piece of art and immediately pick it up and start reconstructing it in this way, the potter would likely be offended, because *Kintsugi* is a personal practice. If the potter chooses to have their pot forever broken and move on to a new pot, that's their choice. It's not up to us as onlookers to fix what someone else has that's broken, I don't think. We can love them, help them with their story, but we can't force philosophy. Because it rarely, if ever, works and can actually often become more detrimental.

I'm the guy who likes being quick to recognize a broken pot and quick to want to help people find some gold lacquer to fix it. Some of you might argue that me even writing this out is an attempt at that. If it's not your pot that's broken, I don't think it's your business to apply the lacquer; this is something I had to work through with Jimmy and has been an ever-present part of other relationships in my life, one of which involves Emily and the passing of her mother.

But this problem of being quick to try and find solutions isn't just in things as extreme as the loss of a loved one. There are broken pottery pieces all around. Big and small. As participants in life with those who've encountered such shattered states, we have to walk at their pace. And sometimes we have to walk back to them in order to do so.

Branches

One of my first memories of Ryan Miller is of him choosing to order pear soda at a coffee shop. Which, now that I know him, pretty much sums Ryan up in one action. Coffee shops and fancy coffees are the offices and fuel for the millennial pastor. Ryan drinks pear soda. Which is just different enough, with just enough flare, just unique enough, to not be like everything else.

. . .

When I transitioned churches, I did so largely because I was following a girl around. This girl being Emily. Which is a painfully cliché thing for a young Christian male to do, making it an even more painful thing to write out on paper. I had been going to Vineyard 509 for a good while, and I was highly connected to the community. I would preach there from time to time. But I felt it was time for a change, and Emily was a great conduit to get me to that change. Emily went to a place called Branches, a church with minimalist style and a hip name. I was cynical at first.

But during the music at the beginning of the service, the screen had quotes from Peter Rollins and Richard Rohr and Mary Oliver. And then the pastor got up and gave a whole sermon outlining a Japanese parable about the wind and the sun and comparing it to love and Jesus. It seemed that it was a talk that, if I could've drawn up my very best metaphor and my very best stage presence, I would have delivered myself.

And so, I contacted the pastor to meet up for coffee, and he ordered a pear soda.

. . .

Ryan and I are similar. We love to talk about the different ways of seeing God... and how you don't really see God at all... because God is more of what was there all along that you finally recognize through some profound type of encounter... and then, when you try and grasp it, whatever it was that you had labeled as God, it slips away into some new and different beautiful form...

I had just told him about my firefly and spider metaphors. And Ryan, as Ryan does, gave a wonderfully clear illustration of a metaphor he used to talk about the same thing. Which clued us in, yet again, to how even though our definitions of God were abstract, we were tapping into the same general idea. And that idea was mysticism. Metaphor. Mystery. Whatever you want to call it.

Ryan loves to run. He talks about it on stage. He talks about it in person. That being said, Ryan uses a lot of running illustrations. And his particular illustration similar to my firefly one centered around an experience he had on one of those runs.

Here in Spokane, we have a mountain that to a midwesterner is a mountain, but to a Pacific Northwesterner is a hill. I'm the former of the two by birth, hence my label. It's called Mount Spokane, and it is northeast of town.

Ryan's story goes that one day he was running on this mountain, through the forests and on the trails that teeter up and down in elevation. He came to a spot in a clearing where the wind was blowing in such a forceful way, the kind of way that is so forceful you can't do anything but just stand your ground and encounter it. Similar to a big wave in the ocean, you are helpless, but in a beautiful way.

Ryan wanted to remember this wind and save it because of the amazing feeling it generated in him. He emptied his water bottle and opened the lid and held it up to catch some of the wind.

That following Sunday on stage he told this story. He told everyone that because it was so profound for him, he wanted to share it with everyone else. So, he had brought the water bottle with him.

"Okay guys, so here it is. Just let this take over you. Just feel it and experience it," Ryan said, with his hand about to twist open the lid.

And, as you probably guessed, when Ryan opened the bottle, no wind came rushing out. Because you can't capture the wind. Ryan equates wind to God. Because wind is an experience, something that is powerful, profound, and, at times, helplessly beautiful. For thousands of years, people have been trying to talk about God and show God to other people. We've written about God (is this not what the Bible, the Qu'ran and other sacred texts are?), we listen to sermons on God, we have genres of music about God. But a bottle can't contain the wind,. And none of these things can contain the reality of what it is that we experience when we truly experience something Divine. You have to encounter that reality yourself.

Perhaps the most interesting thing is how encountering it almost always happens when you least expect it. When you feel helpless and alone. When you are at your most weak.

The wind is free-flowing, *can't* be harnessed, and *can* appear anywhere and everywhere that has not been corrupted by human parameters. These same characteristics are the way of whatever Divine reality is. Every title that tries to give Divinity a definition or a house always fails at some level. Because you know what houses, or any structure, closed off to the reality of the world does? They block the wind. Just like a jar kills off the firefly and its light.

The point has never been to catch God. The point has been to encounter whatever God is. And that largely doesn't happen in the container-based categories we set for divine things, but more through going about our life open to the way of wonder.

. . .

If Mindy was the one to help show me the way of Christ in a new way during my college years, Ryan was the one to inspire me to turn that understanding of the way into tangible reality. And by tangible and reality I literally mean things people can hold. Like this book in your hands. While pastoring Branches, Ryan also ran two graphic design companies with his wife Heidi, 08Left and Mango Ink. Their love for graphics was inspired by a love for creation. And Ryan has mastered the art of taking an idea and giving birth to it. He follows the rule of Seth Godin, which is to *ship it,* meaning just get your ideas out there. And time and time again Ryan told me the importance of recognizing the reality of making things *good enough* rather than perfect. He saw perfection as a form of fear.

And he lives this. He has written multiple books, has created multiple companies, has started a church, and is always creating the *next thing*. Ryan recently told me he was stepping away from Branches for this purpose; he wants to start doing something new. To create new pathways. He's leaving his job and security in pursuit of creativity. The inspiration something like that yields is tangible, especially when you are around Ryan. He's just different enough to spark intrigue, but not so different he's pretentious or unapproachable.

He drinks pear soda in coffee shops.

Death Valley

Growing up, my family went to a church called Kensington. We started attending when I was in fourth grade. One of the first things I did independently that was tied to this church was go on a retreat to a camp in northern Michigan. While I was there, I happened to create a friendship with a kid named Jeff, who just so happened to be the son of Kensington's founding pastor, Steve Andrews. Kensington has, at least last I checked, six campuses and thousands of attendees every weekend. It is one of, if not the, largest churches in the Detroit area.

I didn't really keep in contact with Jeff after the weekend trip, but I am still friends with Steve today. Throughout high school, and when I'd come home from college, Steve, my Dad, and I would play golf, or I would go talk theology with Steve in his office. We tracked with each other. No question was out of bounds for him. And even if Steve may not be as interested in some of the more progressive theology I was intrigued by, he would listen and not interject.

However, as I grew older my distaste for Kensington as a church grew as well. Part of it stemmed from what I mentioned earlier. I had questions not always seen as okay within the framework of the setting of their youth group. Yet through all of this, Steve and I, even as my cynicism for his church grew, remained good friends.

The summer between my junior and senior years of college, my family had dinner with Steve and his wife, Paula. They had been to Death Valley the previous summer, and all they were talking about were the flowers. Which seemed a bit counterintuitive to me seeing as Death Valley is known for its dryness and lack of life. Hence the name Death Valley. But what Steve and Paula shared is that once every ten or so years, Death Valley has a super bloom. Which is just as mesmerizing as it sounds.

. . .

Life can be dry and dormant and dehydrated of all that gives us hope. Leaves can be replaced by dust and streams replaced by dried-up riverbeds. We're not always living in the oasis. Sometimes the ground we stand on stretches for miles—dusty and lacking any sign of flourishing.

Life can be like Death Valley.

Death Valley averages 2.36 inches of rainfall per year. It has the hottest temperature ever recorded at a measly 134 degrees. The ground can reach temperatures of 201 degrees —11 degrees less than the temperature at which water boils. As its name suggests, it's a valley full of death. Cracked ground stretching for miles on end. Sand. Barrenness.

Just like our lives at times.

There can be days and weeks and months and seasons where the nourishment we need to keep going seems distant, perhaps even impossible to grasp. The hopelessness and hardship and heaviness of reality can make mirages of the things off in the distance that we are searching for, or what we thought was reality, or what we had been working towards. There are times when we can feel stuck and stagnant and incapable in our lives.

But through all of these difficulties, little pieces of potential have a habit of nestling themselves into the barren places of our given situations.

The ghost of the wind embraces the emptiness of Death Valley. And with the ghost's invisibility comes the manifestation of tiny pieces of the physical world. Seeds. The beginning stage of a wildflower's life distributed across soil often unfit for sustainability. But they are there nonetheless. Waiting through the heat and unending days where potential seems impossible.

Throughout our hardship—the days where we are surrounded by bad news and failure and disappointment—there's always something sliding itself into the reality of what we face. Little pieces of insight and lessons. Seeds of the wisdom to come. Invisible without hope, but being distributed by an Insistence, that, like the wind, we can't see but is always moving and spreading seeds of what will grow in time.

And that time for Death Valley is during the *super bloom*. An event every ten years or so, when the place of unending brown becomes clothed in vibrant colors.

The rarity of rain seeps itself into the hard ground, paving the way for life to spring forth. And what was once a vast nothingness turns into a canvas of all that had been waiting to be seen for some ten-odd years. All of this occurring through the process of taking time to give the needed nourishment to those seeds. The seeds that had been hiding in the cracks through the unending hot days.

When things are difficult—when life gets hard—when death seems to be all we know—

There are seeds being dispersed.

Pockets of potential that might not sprout right away, but eventually grow and become the colors representing all that we've learned and all that the hard days have taught us. Difficulty is not something that we can take a prescription for. It's a journey through the often-frustrating process of experience. But through all experience there comes wisdom; always being distributed, even if we don't see it at the time.

And just as the wind distributes seeds even on the *hottest* days, so too does wisdom distribute itself through our experience—even, and perhaps most notably, on our *hardest* days. And in due time those days are the ones we often grow from the most. The life lessons learned become a part of the beautiful canvas that is the independent experience of our lives. We see the wildflowers as beautiful because of the stagnancy they have taken the place of. That being said, the hard times are never something to make light of because of what is coming. The hardship is real. It stings. It hurts.

But through it all there are seeds. Remember the parallels the Hebrew people drew to breath and wind and God? To them, the Divine was something always on the move. Distributing lessons and love and hope anywhere and at any time. Even if on some days it was to varying degrees. The wind is spreading seeds in Death Valley. Spirit is spreading seeds in our lives.

Sometimes a seed has to wait a while to receive the water that will turn it into the wildflower it will eventually become. But even the driest place in the world gets rain sometimes.

. . .

Steve is one of the seeds buried in the dust of resentment tied to my past context for spirituality. Places, such as Death Valley and churches, can be rather lacking in the life department. But each person is a seed. And although you may not see them initially, although they may be hiding in the depths of where the resentment resides, they too can bloom.

Although I still am not a huge fan of everything Kensington does, the bitterness has slowly begun to slither itself into the form of beautiful new life. My youth group leader and I,

Justin, had a huge falling out that summer of my senior year. I threw all my frustrations at him. Mercilessly. He expressed himself back. It got ugly. There was some serious pain on both sides.

But over the past few years, when I've gone home, I've occasionally met up with him. We've made amends. He wrote me a letter for my wedding. There is camaraderie there again, even if we don't talk all that much.

Love doesn't necessitate agreement. Nor does dormancy necessitate a lack of potential. I have found that everything blooms in time and everything dies in time and that this happens over and over again. But that is the beautiful reality of seasons. The cycle is never over. The true challenge is learning to love people and reality, at least to some extent, in every stage people and reality present themselves.

Dirt - A Grounded Theology

It was early May, Kylie and I were sitting around trying to find a way to end the year for our small group leaders and their small groups. We wanted there to be a communal opportunity for everyone to do something together. We wanted it to be fun. We wanted it to be reflective. And we wanted it to end with s'mores.

Which made Whitworth's Back 40 the perfect location. It had space for some interactive spirituality. The Back 40 was given its rather unoriginal name because it is exactly what it says it is—the forty acres behind campus. So, Kylie and I decided we would use the Back 40 as the host site for an interactive prayer walk, allowing those involved in the spiritual life of Oliver Hall to engage their five senses. The Back 40 has a smoke shack with a fire pit to grill s'mores. And, perhaps most importantly, it has a lot of dirt. And dirt was exactly what I needed to impart my last little lesson of the year—that we are all a bunch of dirtbags.

. . .

This statement, done to yield the intentional dramatic effect it likely yielded, requires a bit of background. And that background begins with the newfound fascination I had with the ground that spring. On one of my many walks in the Back 40, I began to become a bit more aware of what was accompanying me on every step that I took—the ground beneath my feet. That ground, while at times being pavement, or grass, or gravel driveway, was always supported by dirt. And that simple fact started to bend my mind a bit.

This was all happening during the period of spring when the ground had thawed just enough to where you can scoop up a handful of soil. But when you do, the dirt blankets your palm with an icy chill. This is exactly what I began to do on these walks. I'd pick up the dirt and rub it into my hands furiously. Emily and I were dating at this point. And when I would come over to her house to make dinner together, she would wonder why my hands were so dirty. It was as if I had become her nuisance of a toddler rather than her boyfriend. She likely regretted asking, because the answer I gave was a five-to-ten-minute rant explaining how fascinating dirt is.

I began to realize that just as dirt bonded all of the ponderosa pines and dandelions and grasses of the Back 40 together, it bonded the whole scope of people on my theological spectrum together too. And this was largely inspired by a conversation I had with my housemate Adam at Moody.

Adam was pleased to tell anyone and everyone he met that his name was, "Adam, but you can call me dirt boy."

Adam was not in love with dirt (were you, Adam?) but he was in love with jokes pertaining to Hebrew translations. And, if you look back at the creation story in Genesis, the opening book of the Bible, Adam's name means dirt being. In that creation account, if you are unfamiliar, God scoops up the dirt and breathes (breath = spirit, remember?!) into the dirt to make a human. Humans then, by this account, are a combination of the physical, dirt, and the spiritual, breath. According to Genesis, we are all a bunch of bags of dirt. Or, for comedic effect, dirtbags.

But if the only way you could see how dirt can bond all of humanity together, like it bonded the plants of the earth, is through the scope of a single religion's creation account, it didn't really bond all of humanity together. Enter theoretical physicist and, even if he wouldn't say so, poet Lawrence Krauss.

Krauss talks about how all matter, if we look at the world through the lens of the big bang theory, is a by-product of stardust. That being true, every atom in your body is a by-product of the same type of dust as the dirt you track into the house after a long day outside. You and dirt are cosmic brothers and sisters.

So, whether you are a hard-core, conservative Christian creationist, or a hard-core atheist, the one thing you can both agree on is you are both dirtbags. But we've gotten way from this ancestry.

Dirt lets all things in, cultivating life in so many diverse plants!

But we can be divisive.

In one tablespoon of dirt, you'll find ten billion organisms!

But we can be narrow-minded.

. . .

The prayer walk asked each leader and their small group members to interact with each of their five senses. And when it came to the sense of touch, the walk asked them to pick up a handful of dirt and smear it on their hands, creating a postgardening effect. In doing this, you see just how well paired we are with the earth in the way that the dirt seeps into every pore. Almost becoming one with your skin.

For the sense of sight, we asked participants to look around at the ponderosa pines and the needle-blanketed ground. And in doing so, truly see the complexity of commonality.

Next, in the hearing phase, we asked everyone to listen to the birds and the wind in the trees. The Spirit making its way through our lives overhead. Something so Persistent yet the thought escapes us so quickly.

The fourth stage was smell. It was interacted with via the pine needles and the memories the needles would generate. Participants were invited to contemplate how scent invites us to a place of the past. Yet it is also the sense that leads to anticipation through it's triggering of our salivating glands. We are caught somewhere between past and future every time we interact with smell. And this middle-ground is accessed through the practice of entering into the now.

And then there was taste, which was experienced through the act of consuming s'mores. And the reading of Psalm 34:8. And invites more commentary.

Taste

The most intimate of the mystical experiences, seems to be taste, in which we receive, so to speak, the kiss of God in our inmost being. - Father Thomas Keating

In the Bible, or more accurately in certain spheres that talk about the Bible in certain ways, there's a lot of talk about the gnashing of teeth. It's supposed to generate an image of hell. Weeping. Teeth gnashing. Add the fire and fury imagery of Dante, and you've got yourselves the perfect thing to scare people into conversion.

I was with my friend Kent at Subway, talking with Emily and a few other young folks. Young folk being all of us except Kent, who was the wise elder. Kent is a professor at Whitworth; a bit of a firebrand, a prophet, and a pain in the ass for conservatives. He's a progressive thinker. And he likes diving past assumptions.

We had all been at the same Branches service where Ryan

had been talking about a parable. The parable with the buckets of gold, where the one individual who doesn't multiply their gold is banished out of heaven by God to spend their time—

Weeping and gnashing their teeth.

It's important to recognize that the banishment of this individual was because they didn't chose to be open to what happened to their riches. They were closed off to something new or something open.

Kent has studied both Greek and Hebrew, and Greek happens to be the language the New Testament was predominantly written in (or Aramaic for those academics keeping track at home). It was his study of Biblical languages that led Kent to offer a new insight on the word gnashing that I found compelling.

Typically seen as beating over and over again, a gruesome image to be sure, gnashing, in light of the the original languages definition, has a better translation that means to set one's jaw against. Gnashing really just means having clenched teeth, like a dog gets when it's when angry. There's so much animosity and defensiveness that the dog clenches its jaw and stands on guard. These clenched teeth signal that the dog is setting itself apart from whatever may be approaching it.

We, humans, do this too, even if unconsciously. We clench our teeth when anxious or defensive or frustrated.

This idea of clenching our teeth is a whole different idea of hell than the one we typically have in our mind. That idea, the one we typically think of, is all about fire and burning and torment. But that isn't all that Jesus of an idea, quite frankly.

For Jesus, hell is weeping. And weeping is often associated with shame.

For Jesus, hell is a clenched jaw. And that usually means being on the defensive or having pent-up animosity.

Those living in a hell-like state are typically those who feel too ashamed to encounter the love of God. Or those whose teeth are clenched in such a defensive way that they can't—

Taste.

Psalm 34:8 has an interesting stance on taste. According to it, we taste to know God. Taste and know the goodness of the Lord is what it says. And one thing we most certainly cannot do with a clenched jaw is taste.

Taste is a vulnerable alignment with openness. It's a willingness to encounter something new, or fresh, or risky. Having a clenched jaw is the complete opposite.

Hell has been a heated topic in the church for centuries, not just recently. It's one of those divisive issues people toss around a lot. And the general notion that I had growing up was if I didn't want to go to hell, I shouldn't do certain things.

The funny thing was the series of *don'ts* that supposedly allowed me to avoid hell happen to be the type of legalism that Jesus actually describes hell as being. Jesus talked about hell as a consciousness or a state built around the notions of shame and an unwillingness to taste. Which is exactly what legalism and dogma breed.

The religion I believed in growing up, and the one presented to me quite frequently at Moody and in a lot of other places of Christian thought, seemed to align people with a posture of shame (I'm not good enough without the blood of Christ) and to being closed off (oh, we definitely don't do or think *that way,* or we don't read *that person* or affirm of *that lifestyle*). When your teeth are clenched, you can't taste. And when you can't taste, you can't encounter the goodness of God. This is a metaphor just as much as it is objective truth.

Growing up, my little brother Colin wouldn't ever eat anything except hamburgers. The only time he changed up his order was by one time asking for a cheeseburger without cheese. Smart-aleck. But then, on a trip where Colin time and time again stood outside his comfort zone by standing on the edge of the Oregon coast cliffs and camping in a tent for the first time, I convinced him to order fried rice. And he loved it.

Stepping outside the realm of the paradigm he viewed as right and okay led to a new type of encounter. Our palettes are direct informants as to the way the God of the universe operates.

When we step out of legalism and open ourselves up to a free and open God, a God similar to a backyard full of fireflies, a God of insistence, a God of water vapor, rather than a God of dogma, we begin to taste a variety of different spices tied to the same overarching Divine reality. We see Him or She or It in places we never thought we'd expect or be able to otherwise.

In other religions.

In people supposedly on the outside.

In the *secular*.

But when we clench our teeth, when we stay closed off from the possibility of life and instead live into dogma and legalism and rules, we live in a state of hell.

At least according to Jesus.

Olives

As a kid I hated olives. I had a hard time understanding how anyone could possibly like those little black orbs of grossness. They came on salads, some people put them on their sandwiches, and uncles popped them in their mouths nonchalantly.

I didn't get it.

How could a piece of food that was so gross be such a fixture in the wider context of cuisine?

Four out of our five senses are relatively passive in nature. We touch without even thinking about it. We see things without trying, they just happen in front of us. I'm in a coffee shop right now, and although I'm not listening to conversations, I am passively hearing them. And I'm also smelling the espresso being brewed.

But taste? Taste is different. Taste requires our active

192

participation.

To taste something is risky because something can taste foul and disgusting. It can make us want to heave and gag and vomit. Colin didn't want to taste anything but hamburgers growing up because the safety that came from knowing what he was getting from the hamburger surpassed the adventure of trying something new.

Throughout my college years, I heard all this brutal stuff that God is associated with in our culture. How, in a lot of people's minds, God is judgmental, obsessed with damnation, in some external realm, demeaning of women, a hater of gays, misguided, and loads upon loads of other things.

God, to a lot of people, tastes terrible. And rightfully so.

But have you ever eaten with someone and they are ranting about how you have to try their food and at first glance whatever it is looks disgusting, and you don't want to try it, but they keep telling you to try it, and then you try it and— it's amazing?

This psalmist is onto something. There is something else that we can taste when it comes to God. Something personal, an understanding that tastes radically different than what was initially handed to us.

This year, after a good ten years of not going anywhere near olives, I tried them again. They were sprinkled on a salad, and, at first, I didn't know they were there. But after I noticed this unique and foreign taste, I looked down and saw them. And much to my surprise, I took another bite of the salad. And another and another and another.

I suddenly liked olives.

What we initially view as gross and a ruiner of good things, what is initially associated with damnation and judgment and hate and being backward, is desperately longing to be redefined. But we first need to encounter that new reality. And all that takes is a simple taste, and the mysterious thing is sometimes that taste happens when we don't even expect it to.

We don't even seek it out; it instead comes to us.

God, to me, for a while at least, was something I couldn't stand. *He* was associated with cheesy youth pastors and straightforward answers to questions that were the furthest thing from straightforward. He was judgmental, mean, and not inclusive. But then, one night, as I drove home from a friend's wedding alone-

Overwhelmed by the feeling of being by myself in the world, listening to the Night Bed's song "Lost Springs," more vulnerable than ever —

I tasted something.

A new something. Something that said,

"You. Yes you. I see you. I feel you. I know you. I'm in you. I'm outside of you. I'm here. I'm close. I'm distant. I'm love. I'm pain. I'm hope. I'm despair.

I am whatever/wherever I happen to be, and I want you to participate in all this mystery with me."

God, all of a sudden, wasn't an institutionalized *existence*. God was now an ever-present and pulsating and pleading *insistence*. It's not that God was suddenly definable for the first time; rather, God was now housed inside of every definition.

God, this spiritual breath of life, was making everything much more beautiful than ever before because now I had the eyes to see what / who / how / why / where God was. Mystery.

I had tasted something I once found foul.

But now I truly saw.

When something is forced on you, like olives were forced on me in shared salads at dinner when I was a kid, they aren't nearly as good as when you naturally happen upon them.

When preconceived notions of God are given to you, it leaves you no room to taste this Divine reality for yourself.

God is inviting all of us to go out and taste. Taste and discover for ourselves the Insistent beauty that God is. To flip your perception. And to be overflowing with the sheer joy that comes from recognizing that something that was once foul, when seen in a new light, a light that is inclusive rather than exclusive, ahead of us rather than behind of us, affirming rather than demeaning, can be wonderful. Wonderfully amazing. Wonderfully mysterious.

Throughout this season of transition in my life, I admittedly ate a lot of food. And I did this because I was hungry. Because that is what you do. Food, like filling up a gas tank or getting a haircut or going out to buy milk, has become a by-product of x happened; therefore y must happen. I have no gas; I must get more. My hair is sloppy; I must get it cut. I ran out of milk; I'm headed to the store. I'm hungry; I will eat.

And if we look at the way the world works there's nothing objectively wrong with this. There were many times throughout college that I wanted a burrito bowl loaded with guacamole from Chipotle, or fry sauce from Bruchi's, or a Redcoat hamburger. We have cravings, and those cravings are satisfied by eating. Lions do it. Apes do it. Worms do it. All of conscious life, at least as far as I know, eat.

But it's one thing to eat something, and it is another thing to taste it.

Taste is an invitation to a consciousness of the most profound nature. And that's why it is taste that allows us to know God. We can all consume words of a book like the Bible, but can we taste the nuances and distinctions tied to the lives that wrote those words down? Life becomes a lot more interesting when it is a process of recognizing the subtleties that make up the whole picture. The ingredients that make up the meal. Rather than it just being the simple act of consuming, blindly, whatever is put in front of us as truth.

Bread and Life and The Bread of Life

"What makes the food that we do at Alinea so interesting on the outside is that we really don't let ourselves say no to an idea." Greg Achatz, Head Chef at Alinea

Ryan from Branches had me watch a documentary about a restaurant called Alinea in Chicago one time. He framed it as an assignment. And what made it an assignment was the objective of watching it through the lens of how to rethink spirituality.

The documentary was an episode of the Netflix show *Chef's Table*. And it was fascinating. It told the story of Greg Achatz, the chef at Alinea, and his amazing ability to come at food in innovative ways. His restaurant found a way to make sugar float in balloon form so people could suck air as a dessert. And then there was this dish that was cooked in front of you, but the food was hidden underneath burning coals so the people sitting at the table thought it was simply a burning center piece at first.

Achatz is an innovator. And the episode was littered with quotes about innovation. His quote above is exactly what I think Ryan intended me to see through watching this episode.

Ryan was a huge help in getting me to recognize that if you have an idea, run with it. No matter how bizarre and absurd it may seem. I had been all about seeing those fireflies, but I wanted to be able to get people to encounter them as well. Or at least find ways to do that. And just as Achatz was good at rethinking the access point for food, I was interested in doing so when it came to God.

At one of the midweek services I put on at Branches, I had people shut their eyes and gave everyone a plastic container. They were given a choice to reach in and taste what was in it or to leave it be. This activity spoke to the whole clenched versus open-mouth idea. If you taste something bad, it's certainly not pleasant, but it goes away. If you taste something good and you enjoy it, you have just opened yourself up to a whole new reality. What they all chose to taste was a strawberry, something all of them enjoyed.

But it was through this newfound interest in food and spirituality intersecting that I began to think about something else. One of the bare basics of food for all cultures. And that was bread.

. . .

Jesus said a lot of weird things. Largely because Jesus was one of those people who spoke in the abstract in order for you to have to wrestle and ponder what it was he was talking about. Which has been happening for over 2,000 years now, so I'd say it worked. But people have turned these abstract statements into concrete dogma, and now people argue about them unendingly. One of the most abstract statements, though, is Jesus's self-description as *the bread of life* that occurs in the sixth chapter of the book of John.

This statement pairs nicely with the communion that was given at the Last Supper, the meal that Jesus had with all of his disciples before he was sentenced to death by the ruling authorities of the time. At this supper, Jesus took an ordinary thing like the meal in front of all the dinner guests, and attributed Himself, to the bread. An abstract dinner guest. What a pain.

"This is my body broken for you. This is my blood shed for you," were his words.

And through this imagery of bread and wine, we now have the sacrament of communion. And just when you think the simple act of eating could be a place where theological quarrel would give itself a break, we see the rise of argument once again. Just as a family argues around the dinner table of pot roast and mashed potatoes, the theologians of history argue at the table of bread and wine.

Catholics say the bread turns into the literal body and the wine turns into the literal blood. Protestants say that's absurd.

But just as those who argue at the table of pot roast and

mashed potatoes miss the taste of the meal, those arguing at the table of bread and wine miss the point of the metaphor. The one about Jesus being the bread of life.

A little while before Jesus came along, there was a guy named Moses. Moses led a group of Israelites out of Egypt and into the Promised Land. Whether or not this story literally happened doesn't seem to matter because the story, literal or not, foreshadowed a metaphor Jesus longed for us to understand. And that metaphor was when the people were desperate and hungry, there was bread, the sustenance needed for life, to be had. And this bread came in the form of manna, a middle eastern style of bread. Wandering around aimlessly for years and years and years can leave your stomach pretty empty, so manna was a helpful change of pace from the locusts and worms these Israelites were likely eating. And the Jewish people saw the manna as a gift from God.

The interesting thing about bread is that almost every people group has some variation of it. There's manna for the Jews. There's mantou for the Chinese. There's naan for the Indians. There's the baguette for the French. There are the tortillas of Latin America. There's the fry bread of Native American cultures.

There's a lot of bread in the world.

And the other interesting thing about bread is that no matter where in the world it is made, it is reliant on nothing more than two ingredients, grain and air.

Grain is physical; it is of the earth. Whether corn or barley or rice, grains are dirty and earthy and grounded. Air is spiritual. It's here, but we can't see it. It's brushing our face, but we can't grab it. It's filling our lungs to keep us alive, but we can't capture it.

Bread, in a sense, is 100 percent physical and 100 percent spiritual. It is air, and it is grain. And it occurs everywhere, in every culture, by many names, and in the context of the life-giving act of communion known as—eating together.

So, when Jesus says he is the bread of life when he compares his body to bread, is he saying that he too is 100 percent physical and 100 percent spiritual? Occurring anywhere? In every culture? By many names? And in the communion of people, like through the act of sharing a meal?

By distinguishing himself as bread, Jesus is tying himself to something intrinsically tied to every culture of the world. And like a firefly outside the jar rather than in, it's not about pinpointing which bread Jesus is, but about tasting the nuances and idiosyncrasies of all the different bread and letting it grow your understanding of—the theme. The way. The truth. And perhaps it's in bread where we find the life.

Healing Prayer

During my freshman year at Moody, Jake and I volunteered at a youth group called Youth for Christ. This organization focuses on youth in the margins of a rough neighborhood in Spokane. Volunteering was part of Moody's educational system, called PCM, which stands for Practical Christian Ministry. Which, for all of the frustrations I held toward Moody, is one thing that's admirable. It helped students live out their education practically.

Jason from the Vineyard church would join Jake and I every week to work with the middle school students. Jake would run around throwing dodgeballs, and I would stand around more awkwardly than any of the middle schoolers, who are, by societies' standards, the staple of such a character trait. Kids flocked to Jake, were curious of me, and were downright confused by Jason. And that confusion only heightened one night when a kid, I think whose name was Nate, showed up with a broken foot.

. . .

Jason is an amazing person. He and his family had moved up to Spokane from Redding in the summer of 2013, right before I arrived myself. They left a community they were highly connected to, job security, and family in order to plant a church.

Jason and his wife, Amber, hail from the Vineyard denomination. Vineyard churches sprung up in a spirit similar to the counterculture movement and were a Christian by-product of the hippy movement. Vineyard churches are known for taking Jesus very seriously, which you would think would be something all Christians do. Vineyard congregants, though, dabble in the area of *red-letter Christianity,* a framework that puts the words of Jesus, often written in red in the Bible, as priority before any other text.

Jesus is important, and so is the Holy Spirit for Vineyard folk. The Vineyard denomination, especially in my experience, believes the Holy Spirit is very much alive in the world. I agreed with this but in much more of a mystical way. Mystical in my case meaning the existence of spirit in metaphor, permeating from all things. Spirit to me, as I've mentioned, is characterized as Persistence. It's the push you feel when you see someone marginalized, the push you feel to intercede on their behalf, the push to be love in the world.

The spirit for Jason and Amber, and the Vineyard denominations and others like it that identify with a word

Christian theology labels as *charismatic*, is a bit more, well...
spooky.

They believe in healing prayer, speaking in tongues, and
casting out demons. Which was a new dynamic for me, and
it pushed me. And I still have trouble with it today. Jason
wanted to go into the neighborhood of our church, knock on
doors to see if people wanted to join us on Sundays, and
then pray for them. This sort of thing was not my form of
faith.

I saw this as creating the all-too-common sin of Christianity
—attempting to place Christ *onto* a given situation, as
opposed to drawing Christ *out of* a situation. The distinction
being that I believe the way of Christ is already inherently
alive everywhere, even if not by that specific title. Others
believe Christ needs to be imparted into people or
situations. My thought process was that God was in all
because love exists everywhere, no matter how broken. And
God is love. So, our job is to seek out that love. Because it's
there somewhere. Which, side note, means that conversion
isn't necessary. People don't need to accept Christ into their
heart, Christ, the Insistence of God, is already there. I'd be
more inclined to say that people are simply invited to align
with that way. A way of love, wonder, hope, compassion,
etc.

All this to say, I didn't want to knock on any doors.

. . .

But, now that we've got my long-winded prefacing out of
the way, let's get back to Nate and his foot. Nate was a little

pain in the ass. Which isn't exactly fair because Nate grew up in a very rough situation. But he was the kid that every week, would yell any obscenity that crossed his mind. Not as a threat, but to see how far he could go before the leaders tossed him out. He would throw stuff at whoever spoke, would spread his food all over the table, and would flirt in a way terrifying to think a middle school kid was capable of.

But Nate's antics had been stifled a bit by a broken foot, so he had stuck around until the breakout session on this particular night. Jake and I had Nate in our group. He and about five other guys filed to a corner room of the Youth for Christ building. Because I was working with Jake, and because Jake was well loved, our group had the majority of the guys who showed up that night. So, Jason joined our group.

"What happened to your foot," Jason asked Nate.

Nate looked up and replied, "I was skateboarding and landed on it funny. The doctor said it's a break of a metatarsal or something."

Nate's eyes avoided contact with Jason's. Jason saw an opportunity for that spirit stuff that creeped me out.

Jason continued, "Well, I believe God can heal that kind of thing if we pray. I've seen it happen. It doesn't always happen but what do you think? Can we pray over it?"

I felt so uncomfortable I didn't know what to do. Jake and I were eyeing each other. Both our eyes saying the same thing, "Why Jason, why?!"

Nate released something from his vocal chords that was in between a scoff and a laugh, combined with a roll of the eyes, which eventually turned into, "That's weird but sure, I guess."

And so, with the Spirit supposedly slowly descending from above, Jason rallied the troops. These troops being 7th graders coming from places of poverty and two college students coming from a place of quiet concern and cynicism, and had all of us descend our hands on Nate's foot.

And then Jason began to pray.

And Nate began to shimmy in his spot on the floor.

And then Jason asked if anything was happening in between the utterances of his intercession.

And Nate replied something confusing and paradigm shfting,

"I, I uh, I feel something like shifting in my foot."

"Good. Good!" Jason replied, "Let's keep going."

And so, through Jason's breath, which is the same word, I always remind people, for Spirit in Hebrew, orthopedic surgery was performed. Because, inexplicably, Nate stood up post-prayer and walked around with no pain. And to hurt the brain even more, he came back the next week with X-rays showing there was no break anymore.

. . .

Cathy, mother of four-year-old Matthew, wife of African immigrant Patrick, grade school music teacher, and attendee of Vineyard 509, died of brain cancer in the summer of 2017.

I was in a phase of leaving the Vineyard church led by Jason and Amber where Cathy also went when she was diagnosed. She was an amazing woman. She led worship every week, was soft-spoken, insightful, and kindhearted. She truly was a gift to be around. And my leaving the church, although because of a few different reasons at the time, was definitely one part flee from grief.

Before I left though, Cathy had many hands placed on her head in prayer for healing. But it didn't work.

It made no sense. How could a woman, an elementary school music teacher, mother, and wife not be healed by prayer from something that would eventually kill her, but a kid who broke his foot skateboarding could?

When I was in high school, my grandfather got really sick. He was in the ICU, and we thought he was a goner. Countless people were praying for him; I asked friends to pray via text, social media posts, word of mouth. You know the drill. And in the middle of the night, he woke up in the ICU. His first impulse was to pull the tracheal tube out of his throat because it was uncomfortable, and then asked to be released. Just months later he was back to playing golf.

My wife Emily's mother suffered from bipolar disorder. She was unbelievably loved by Emily and Emily's dad, sister, brother, and countless others. She was prayed for by so many for years and years. She ended up passing because it took hold of her too greatly.

There are so many stories we hear about people getting miraculously healed. It's become a message we hear in churches, to put anything to God and God will respond.

But what about the people who do and witness tragedy anyway? Why is healing from a supposedly loving God a lottery system? And why is asking these types of questions not seen as okay?

Christianity has a repression problem. A problem of creating places that we simply aren't allowed to go within the dominant consciousness of the religion. It's high time we start creating churches that preach about healing one service and then about God seemingly not showing up the next.

I still don't know how I feel about the whole healing prayer thing. I know I've seen it work, and I know I've seen it not work. And I have to say, the pain I've seen in people who have had it not work is often longer lasting and more detrimental than the joy I've seen in the people who have had it work.

Anytime we frame something within the scope of a predetermined expectation, we leave very little room for story to unfold. And the world needs much more space for story. Because it is in the steady revelation of story where meaning is revealed.

The Best Job Title I Could Have Imagined

Toward the end of my junior year at Whitworth, Mindy came to me with the idea of sitting in on Whitworth's student government as a bit of an intermediary between the Chapel and Student Life department. Spiritual programming and student programming seemed to be running parallel to each other and getting each to work in tandem seemed a difficult process. The recognition of this dynamic and desire to do something about it was spearheaded by my buddy John, who had been a part of the student government throughout our junior year.

The idea of an explicitly spiritual voice sitting in on student government meetings felt to some on student government like a pushback to the more forward-thinking tendencies of the government itself. But to others, it seemed necessary to add a voice that was there to speak to the theological at meetings. The way these meetings worked was student representatives for each residence hall, and coordinators from a variety of departments on campus such as athletics, diversity, and sustainability, amongst others, dialogued about policy and its implementation. Events, programming, and stances that represented the student body also were birthed out of these weekly meetings.

The government wanted to test out someone speaking on behalf of the chapel to see if adding this role the following year was worth it. I told Mindy I would try it out and see what came of it.

I would like to believe that by this point in my time at Whitworth, I had built an identity as someone who was very much enamored with discussing things about spirituality. That being said, I was also someone who didn't have these discussions within the confines of the Theology Department. Although I graduated with a theology minor, that was much more a result of all of my Moody credits that I transferred in with. I wasn't really part of the Whitworth theology dynamic. Which was how I liked it after being around such circles at Moody and often finding myself growing cynical. This weird in-between place I found myself in allowed me to speak to the spiritual reality of campus more so than the theological. And there is a distinct difference between the two, especially at an institution of higher learning.

Education and spirituality hold a difficult balancing act at Whitworth, and likely most all other places with these two dynamics at play. The Theology Department existed within the walls of Westminster Hall. And the topics discussed within the theology classrooms were intriguing and interesting, predominantly, to those within the scope of theological education. But to someone with no interest in academic theology, such conversations could occasionally come across as aloof or detached. Because on a college campus and in life, every single person brings their own element of the spiritual. And having a whole department that sought to give definition or attribution to God seemed, even if not intentionally, to negate this a bit.

The spiritual makeup of Whitworth's campus or any campus isn't housed in any particular department. It is more a vapor-like presence existing in all different places on campus. And that's what I wanted to attempt to speak to. The inherent spiritual dynamic at play – not just the theological musings of theological subsets of the campus itself.

This balance of spiritual but not necessarily theological can make people on either side of the issue, those against theology and those for it, mad. But it can also make those on either side relieved and happy as well. And it's in this tension that things often have the greatest opportunity to create an identity because they aren't overly shaped by one influence or another.

After a month or so playing this role as best I could, based on what I thought it should be and chatting with John unendingly regarding his hopes for it, it was decided that a position titled *spiritual life coordinator* would be created for the next year. And I was all about applying for it. For one because the title sounded really cool to me, but also because of how open-ended a job like that could be. And how much freedom it gave to create a melting pot of spiritual experiences for students on a Christian campus.

I got the job. Which meant that my senior year I'd get paid to chat with students about the spiritual nature of campus and to put events on that helped facilitate creative new ways of interacting with that spiritual nature.

. . .

Part of the benefit of working a job that is tied to a topic in which you have tried to identify yourself by is what it does for your ideas. The ideas that I'd had all along now had a conduit to tangibility. A space, to use Mindy's language, for them to have legs.

My job was to coordinate spiritual life on campus, which was an open-ended duty. The job description that John created the previous year for the spiritual life coordinator position was purposefully left open-ended so that whoever held the position could shape it as they saw fit. Most of what was in the job description were checklist items to give the job some structure. Things like meeting with Forrest Buechner, the Dean of Spiritual Life, and the chapel's graduate assistants twice a month. Meeting with Mindy, my former boss that oversaw the small group coordinators, weekly with SGC's to help them or get help from them when it came to programming. Attending ASWU (Associated Students of Whitworth University) meetings every week, and being part of that team through attending retreats and a class once a week where we'd talk about our programming ideas.

But as far as what events I would put on, what events I would sponsor, and what conversations I would choose to promote — that was largely up to me.

The challenge that Mindy and Dayna Coleman-Jones, the faculty member who oversaw ASWU, discussed with me at the tail end of junior year after I got the job, was distinguishing myself from the chapel and from ASWU. Because as they saw it, I wasn't full-on chapel theology guy. But I also wasn't full-on ASWU guy either. This balance also had a lot to do with the campus belief that ASWU was some overwhelmingly liberal entity holding angst at times towards the Christian tradition at Whitworth.

Both of these entities, the Whitworth Chapel and ASWU, carried themselves a bit like metaphors for overly dramatized definitions of the Christian and the secular. Even though when you entered into them, the two entities were nowhere near as black and white as that. Because nothing ever is.

Although framed as a challenge, this tension was the same tension I thought might help with the dynamic to begin with. At this particular time, I was in the spiritual-but-not-religious phase a lot of people go through when rethinking faith. It seems to be the phase people ashamed of their religion but still finding some beauty in it go through. Dayna and Mindy challenged me to try my best to figure out how I would balance the two dynamics we chatted about over the summer before coming back the following fall.

. . .

But that summer was more than just a three month brainstorming session. Emily and I were dealing with the difficult reality of a long-distance relationship. We were 2,000 miles apart. I had gone to Michigan to spend one final summer with my family, working at the same Young Authors Day Camp I had worked at the previous summer. Emily was working at Camp Spalding, an overnight camp north of Spokane that she had grown up going to and had worked at the previous summer. She had little reception and a boyfriend in myself whose family could only provide so much distraction for his anxious mind.

It was rough.

Long distance relationships are brutal. They can tell you a lot about a dynamic. The healthy parts. The unhealthy parts. And one of my unhealthier qualities that I picked up on was how much I tend to stake my own identity in other people. It was painful but beautiful to learn how to love Emily, but also how to love myself.

But there were also wonderful moments that summer. Like Colin and I's construction of a miniature three-hole chipping golf course in the backyard. We built a hole into the side of the ravine, and a tee box on the edge of the creek at the bottom. There was Emily visiting my family in Michigan for the first time. There were the conversations with my mom about God on the back patio. And the golfing with Dad. Eating family dinners with everyone again.

And that was also the summer where I saw the fireflies

again. Without the urge to catch them. Which was the perfect propeller for my job for the next year.

. . .

All of us student leaders got back to campus early that fall for training and a retreat. We all started off as awkwardly cordial. Some people knew each other, and others didn't. It was a bit like summer camp or any other start of a school year. We shared personal stories, came up with a mission statement, and chatted around a campfire.

Around the campfire was where the whole reality of balance the job would call for first became tangible. And it was beautiful. There were people like Christina, who had grown up in a small town Christian family, and Whit, who had been burned by Christians and saw herself as an agnostic, and tons of others somewhere on that spectrum. And we all just talked. Simply and openly.

We talked about life and spirit and heaven and hell. And because of my title, people kept turning toward me for answers or more questions, which was humbling and bizarre and captivating all at once. I was enamored with the fantastic things everyone was sharing. And this night made me realize that my job was really just an act of trying to get people on a wide-ranging spectrum to talk about the same things with each other. Those things could be loss or doubt or politics or nature, because everyone had experience and opinions with/on those things, atheist and conservative Christian creationist alike. I began to understand that spiritual life coordinator is a good title for someone who is spiritual, but it also basically just means coordinating that which is curious or strikes ones curiosity. It means creating spaces where people can become eager to know or learn something. So that became the goal.

From the Ground Up

I mentioned that at the fireside chat there was a girl named Whit. Whit was someone who did not go along with the Whitworth mold at all. She came from a background that used Christian doctrine to justify horrible things done toward her, was estranged from her family, and just had a really difficult past. Whit had gone through a lot and continued to go through a lot throughout senior year.

I knew none of this about Whit initially of course. She and I were in a couple of classes together, worked on a group project or two, and she was mutual friends with my buddy Brayden's girlfriend, Danica. It was ASWU that allowed me to learn a bit more about Whit's story. Seeing as she came from a background of manipulated Christianity to justify an unjust end (a reoccurring negative theme it would seem with organized religion), we had many conversations on the retreat at the beginning of the year centered on her pains from the faith. She was agnostic and had quite a few interesting thoughts on the Christian framework she had been raised in.

But the reason Whit and I hit it off, more than anything else, was that although we were operating within the two *supposedly* separate frameworks of sacred and secular, we tracked with each other on nearly everything. Which is exactly why I add the caveat of *supposedly*. Sacred and secular tend to become very empty words when you seek out nuance.

We both tried our best to value openness. And Whit did so in a truly profound way. Even with having come from a background of abuse in the name of the ideology I, begrudgingly at times, aligned with, she would still hear me out. Openness is both literally and figuratively the access point to a new room of understanding.

And if it was respect that led to a shared openness, it was the natural world that led to our common ground for conversation. Whit studied environmental science and sustainability and I was always trying my best to create a metaphor pertaining to nature in order to explain an idea.

And so, we did the classic thing any two college kids who like talking about their ideas do—we created a college radio show. It was called *From the Ground Up*, a testament to both ecological preservation and spiritual practice. Whit believed that the dirt beneath us was a starting place for all topics of environmentalism and I believed the dirt beneath us was our heritage and a good place to start any conversation on spirituality.

This theme is what followed us throughout the whole show. We spent four weeks talking about the four basic elements of life: earth, wind, fire, and water. Whit would talk about some fun environmental facts and current issues pertaining to each of our topics, and I'd tie that into a spiritual metaphor. And although Whit wasn't always quick to buy into these spiritual metaphors, she would clue me in on if the metaphor was accurate and respectful of the science. We'd both find songs that spoke to the messages of our shows and used those songs as springboards to more conversation.

And you know what the coolest part was? Not once did we argue.

Not a single time.

Because Whit and I believed the same things, the only thing getting in the way was the terminology of ideology. And yet we live in a world where the dominant narratives are about how Christians are all about conversion and atheists are all out to disprove God.

And it's all such bullshit.

Because you can be an atheist and be a far better Christ follower than Christians, and you can be a Christ follower and be a far better scientist than someone who acts on bitterness to disprove a spiritual ideology. It always comes back to the motivation. A motivation for understanding will always promote unity, and a motivation for opposition will promote division. Conversion should never be the goal. Alignment should. And you can align with love and understanding without converting to an ideology supposedly all about it. And that alignment, I would argue at the end of the day, is all that matters.

. . .

Recently I got a text from Whit. She joined the Peace Corps and moved down to Paraguay to help promote sustainable agriculture in a rural village. Naturally. So cool.

She's been studying the soil to find proper agricultural processes again, studying something *from the ground up* is still applicable in her line of work, in a very tangible way. But another thing she's had to learn is Guaraní, the language of the indigenous people she lives amongst. And their name for person just so happens to be *yvyipora*. *Yvy* meaning dirt. *Ipora* meaning spirit.

Whit, while studying dirt in the most tangible and helpful of ways, just so happens to be seen by these people as they see all the rest of humankind.

As a dirt spirit.

Because as our show sought to articulate, the scientific and the spiritual are never in opposition.

A Poet's Purpose

When I was a senior in high school, I took an AP Literature course taught by Mr. Chisnell. English had always been my subject of choice, and I had been fortunate to have had two amazing teachers in high school that helped lead to my love of English prior to taking Mr. Chisnell's class. I had Mrs. Morello freshman year. She taught me all about metaphor and how metaphor is part of our lives. That idea floored me. I began to seek it out daily, and still do to the best of my ability.

And then there was Ms. Karolak. She is likely in the top five on my list of people who have had the biggest influence on my life. I had her for Honors English sophomore year and AP Writing and Composition junior year. She was the one who introduced me to Thoreau and Emerson and the Romantic period of writing. The nature lovers and *seers* of the world. She helped me truly begin to see and engage with the world instead of passively witnessing it. A differentiation highlighted in the following quote by Ralph Waldo Emerson that was on a bookmark she gave me after I graduated,

"The invariable mark of wisdom within a man is to see the miraculous in the common."

In the height of our discussion of transcendentalism in Ms. Karolak's class, likely talking about how Thoreau was a participator who observed, and Emerson as an observer who participated, I chimed in to offer my two cents on the characteristics of what bound them together.

"What both of them are trying to say is, we are so anxious to gain in this life, that we forget to acknowledge."

At this point, Ms. Karolak beelined it to the chalkboard, picked up a stick of the white stuff, and asked me to repeat myself.

"Uh, I think I said, 'We are so anxious to gain, we forget to acknowledge.'"

As her hands traced out the phrasing of my quote, as I began to feel the odd sort of satisfied uncomfortableness that comes from teacher-given affirmation in high school, and as my friend Trey nudged me, snickering, a newfound sense of ability in the realms of transcendental philosophy was born within me.

"Leave it to Mike to lead us down a new path," Ms. Karolak said. And as she stepped away from the board, there sat my quote, with my initials and the date etched next to it. The quote remained on the board for at least the next two weeks. Which led to a new sense of confidence in academic ability, a profound love for writing and ideas, and in a roundabout way, the mindset that my voice was important. It's amazing and beautiful the impact teachers can have on us.

. . .

This affirmation of my English ability continued sophomore and junior year while in Ms. Karolak's class. And it led to me think that presenting the lyrics to a song I liked to my AP Literature class, the one taught by Mr. Chisnell, was a reasonable and praiseworthy thing to do. The song was painful and was caked with emotion, like a lot of the more classic poems we had been reading.But Mr. Chisnell wasn't someone eager to write his students quotes on the board. He was a man with a strict view of what was literary and what was not. So what was seen as reasonable and praiseworthy to me, to Mr. Chisnell, was not.

The song was called "Sprout," and it was by a Seattle artist named Bryan John Appleby. Trey and I, the same Trey who nudged me two years earlier as my quote was etched on the board, and the same Trey who captained the high school hockey team we both played on, had just read it to the class and now stood in front of Mr. Chisnell with clammy hands.

"Hmm, interesting choice," the man with a gap-toothed smile said in a way that made interesting synonymous with "I'm gonna make you punk hockey players regret this."

Trey and I looked down at our, admittedly, scribbled-the-last-second questions to lead the class in a discussion.

"Okay so first question, guys. What do you think Bryan means when he pairs the lines, 'We all knew that she should've slept until mid-December. When it comes to the lot I have learned, I can't count on the cast.'"

Some girl named Emma raised her hand and said something about how the artist seemed to have learned not to expect what is normal in his life. Reading more into the song lyrics, she guessed that things didn't work out for him much.

Emma's response was accurate with our own reading. We then talked about lines like "baptized in the rolling dark waters of doubt," something Mr. Chisnell was making me feel about my Christian faith that year, with his rants about Mithras and other tales pointing to the often overlooked aspects of religion for us in the west. We talked about the line of "A vision of a father looking on, as he burns to the ground the house that he made." Everyone, with a bit of help from Trey and I, was beginning to realize that the poem was about a miscarriage, and how it led the narrator to lose his faith.

And even though it seemed that the only thing Mr. Chisnell wanted out of us students that year was losing our faith through all the theories he presented to shift our paradigms, he didn't receive our reading of the song as fondly as the rest of the class. He said something like the following,

"I don't see how you could've thought this was acceptable to present. We have been going through an anthology with the likes of Frost, Browning, Keats, Whitman, and other greats. Have you not learned what it is that makes a poem stand out as a great?"

It seemed Mr. Chisnell was using us as an example of what he had argued postmodernism was doing to literature and truth in general—making all of it a level playing field where greatness was increasingly difficult to discern. And although I understood his ploy, I also thought very highly of the ornateness of Appleby's lyrics. I saw this critique as one based on opportunity, rather than actuality. Who's to say Appleby won't be regarded the same way someday, I wanted to say, perhaps ignorantly, perhaps hopefully. But it was no use. Mr. Chisnell's mind was made up. And his mind certainly wasn't compelling him to write a takeaway to be put up on the board for the next two weeks like Ms. Karolak.

Trey and I, wearing our dapper hockey game day attire, sulked back to our seats. I sweat from embarrassment more the rest of that hour than I did during the game later that night.

. . .

Mr. Chisnell, in hindsight, allowed me to grow as a human and set me up to be able to reevaluate my Christian faith. And in that sense, I'm grateful for the time I had in his class. But I carried animosity of that day and frustration towards Mr. Chisnell for a while, even if unconsciously. Music and lyrics were a huge part of my spiritual formation. So, four years later, out of spite and also because said spite graciously chose to align with what I saw as a campus spiritual need, I invited Bryan Appleby to perform at

Whitworth University. And, ironically, the frame for the event was for Bryan to perform Sprout and other songs of his in the same vein and talk about the experience they spoke to. A very similar experience Trey and I tried to speak about on his behalf four years earlier in that tense high school english classroom.

What We Do with Our Doubt

Bryan Appleby and I were walking across the Back 40 at Whitworth. We were carrying a wooden frame with a 9-foot-by-12-foot canvas staple gunned to it. This huge blank sheet would soon become the place for people to respond to the night's event. About three hours or so from this moment, my first program as the spiritual life coordinator was happening. And Bryan was the focal point.

Ever since the painful presentation of "Sprout" during my senior year of high school, Bryan's music had captivated me and was a consistent favorite I would go back to. There was something in his lyrics that seemed to point to a faith-influenced past, but also a falling out from it. "Sprout" highlighted that reality in its lyrics, but so did lots of other songs from his first EP and then again on his first full-length album.

When Bryan's second full-length album, *The Narrow Valley*, came out, I read in an interview that it was an allegory for leaving the faith / worldview / frame of mind you (he in this case) had been brought up with.

The album is a story about a rural coastal town in California, much like the one Bryan told me he grew up in. The town experiences an earthquake, and people have to leave. And as painful as the departure is, they realize, after the fact that it was for the best all along.

For Bryan, it was a departure from Christianity to an agnostic-atheistic humanism that freed him. Moving past his Christian upbringing, not because of a personal hostility he had toward it, but because he found it confining, proved to make him feel much more free.

Later that night, as Bryan, my housemate John, and I were each eight beers deep on my back porch, standing, occasionally stumbling, we were able to put it all in perspective.

We realized then that we were both by-products of waking up to our own frustration with ideologies indoctrinated into us as youth. And although Bryan may have become an atheist, and I a more open Christ-centered mystic, I found we were far more alike than a lot of Christians I was associated with at the time.

And this type of realization that we had after the event was actually the goal of the event itself. To help show ideology isn't always what binds people. It's the story. And even though not all of us share the same ideology, we all have a story. And the more we lean into those, the less emphasis and importance we tend to give the ideology.

. . .

I am a firm believer that art is what gives people an outlet to be authentic. And within my setting, I was a firm believer that students at Christian institutions, namely my institution, weren't able to be authentic about their faith nearly enough. Bare feet and bandanas, coffee one-on-ones, and attending Tuesday's chapel service were the signs of Jesus at Whitworth. And if none of these were ascribed to you, you likely felt outside the norm of the Christian sphere.

The same lyrics that Trey and I analyzed back in high school from Bryan's song "Sprout" really pushed me to do this event. The song, as I mentioned previously, seems to be about beginning to question your faith. Bryan's line about him being "baptized in the rolling dark waters of doubt" points to a new sort of baptism. One that an honest person raised by a specific and closed system tied to a religious ideology likely has to go through if they want to be personal and honest about their faith. We all question when we approach life honestly.

But then questioning takes on a whole other dimension when you're baptized in the "rolling dark waters of doubt," and those waters don't want you to be doubting. This, in my experience at least, is often the case in the Christian sphere. In such situations, where honesty produces doubt, it's no wonder a person may feel like they are drowning. And it's no wonder, if caught in this dynamic, there's often the urge for something new.

The way in which faith communities often deal with doubt is

by avoiding or repressing it. Which is why bringing in Bryan to talk about just how freeing it can be to be real about your faith was important to me. Especially because, as I mentioned, there tended to be a bit of a culture around being a good person of faith on campus. And being that good person largely centered around appearing you and your faith had it all together. Which isn't fair for those who need room to wrestle and... doubt.

The event was all about showing how freeing something like losing what you feel bound by can be. How much more you can breathe when you acknowledge uncertainty. And how it's okay if the result of that honesty is walking away from it all. Because in walking away because of honesty, you would likely be more in line with God's love than you would be if you were to carry on living a lie you forced yourself to believe. Living like that isn't so much a way of freedom as it is shame-ridden indoctrination. And if my experience is true, there's not much freedom tied to shame.

Marketing the concert was rather difficult, however. Especially with holding a title like "spiritual life coordinator." It could be argued that organizing an event that could lead to an existential crisis centered around doubt of one's faith is right in line with the job description of one who coordinates all things spiritual. But that version of the job description is not exactly the description the campus chaplain, Forrest, had in mind.

To get my event announced, I might have made it seem, just slightly, like Bryan had come back to the faith. I never said he did, I more just hinted that he came out of his doubt to see things in a new light. This new light, however, was not *the light of the world* known as Jesus that many saw as being the only way, but more accurately the light Bryan found via abandoning the ideology of that *light* altogether.

But light being as light is, taking its various forms via various conduits, the event was announced nonetheless.

. . .

As I mentioned briefly, the reason that Bryan and I, only a couple of hours earlier, were lugging a 9-foot-by-12-foot frame is that I, along with millions of others, believe art to be a means of allowing us to process in a way we normally wouldn't. And with a 9-foot-by-12-foot canvas located behind the building of the event, lit up by Christmas lights, and with assorted paints scattered about, people would have a chance to artistically process through what Bryan's music had evoked within them. And as the concert began, it was becoming clear that that canvas was about to get crowded.

As Bryan worked through his doubt clad days via songs from his first full-length album, *Fire on the Vine*, I was wiggling in my seat a bit. His performance was perfect. And his voice carried through Whitworth's art building magically. But when he opened up the floor for a Q&A response about his journey and the first question came from some girl who asked him a question riddled with a defensive theology for Christianity, I felt sick. She, clearly, did not take kindly to Bryan's subtle critique. A critique, I may add, that came from Bryan's personal life experience. Not ideological assumptions.

The event was doing exactly what I wanted it to. But my palms were sweating from the awkward sense of tension.

My peers had to do what we as humans don't like to do—doubt. And it wasn't theoretical doubt; this was the doubt of a real person who was performing right in front of us, laying his heart out on the line. A guy who left the faith, not because of animosity he had toward the people of the religion, but simply because he just didn't like the dissonance his life had with its major teachings. And you can't counter someone's life experience with argumentative theology. And that's what people seemed to want to do.

All this, on top of the fact that it was early November and the days were short and it was raining outside created quite the heavy environment.

And then it happened. Bryan, God (an atheist? God? Yes.) bless him, closed the set with the song "Glory." The one he and I had talked about earlier that day as we walked around campus before the rain came in. The song describing the elusive thing he said he still can appreciate when the sun catches his face. Or when he has a good conversation with someone. Or when he realizes the human ability to connect. And in it, there's the line,

"Glory, you are the only mystery I can't seem to solve."

It was that, and Bryan's closing plea to ask questions and to stay curious, that left people to find their paintbrushes and start painting on the canvas outside.

. . .

As people were painting, there were a lot of things going on the canvas that made me realize Bryan had yielded some serious existential questioning in the minds of the students in attendance. People were quiet and painting. Reflective. Some maybe even stoic. Bryan was talking to a number of students. One of the chapel worship leaders was so excited about Bryan's authenticity through art, which was neat to see. And another girl who was agnostic said the event was one of the first times where she felt that she had a voice on on campus. That's what it was all about.

No one seemed mad; everyone just seemed to be wrestling. Like Jacob and God, however many thousand years ago. But Emily was very quiet. I could tell she was mulling something over in her mind. So, before we met Bryan and John at the local bar, Pints, Emily and I would have one of our classic car conversations.

"What's up," I said plainly.

This was met by a very unbelievable "Nothing, really" from Em.

Knowing the conversation needed more unraveling, I continued into it. Discovering, in the process, that my hoped-for existential crisis for students had infected the one student I loved most—Emily.

"The questions he had about faith were really good. Like they weren't just the ones I had easy answers too. It's unsettling. I don't like thinking about that kind of thing,"

Emily said shakily.

It was then that I knew, or rather felt reaffirmed in what I already knew—that my someday-wife and I's faiths were radically different. And it wasn't troubling in the slightest. It instead was reassuring. Because the difference was that Emily is focused on the matter of things. The way of them. Not so much the ideas. Something I need with being someone always stuck in idea land. She makes things matter, tangibly.

The conversation reached no resolution. It was left in the air, just as the doubt of all of Bryan's music was left in the air and manifested on the canvas cloth behind the Whitworth art building. It had been an event on a Christian campus that didn't make you feel cozy at the end but urged people to move towards the reality that dissonance is not always the enemy, and consonance is not always the saint.

Election

There's this thing called a murmuration. It's been on viral videos, and *Planet Earth* highlighted it in their show on cities. The star of a murmuration is the *Starling*, a type of bird in the Sturnidae family. For reasons not quite understood, starlings have a habit of clumping into flocks well into the thousands and soaring through the air in such profoundly beautiful and synchronous ways that what was a clump of thousands of individual birds becomes one giant black series of waves in the sky. It's profoundly beautiful. If you look up "starling murmuration" online, you'll likely find some videos.

The interesting thing about starlings is that there are probably more of them in the United States than there are any other types of bird. They really are nothing special. But when they chose to unify and move in time with one another, they are beautiful and grab our attention.

There are a lot of people who are *for* love in the world. But in 2016, the election results appeared to speak to the contrary. But there still are. I would venture to guess that there are more of us for love than any other type of person in the United States. More than Democrats. more than Republicans. Because being for love is not a party-line issue. That's the problem with putting all our action and stake in the way a certain ideological system operates. We need to transcend categories and join hands in the theme of love.

But the problem is that all of those party lines and ideological blankets we cozy up under hide us from seeing the other people who align with love in other ideological frameworks. All of us who are for love are like individual Starlings when we sit and mutter around by ourselves or in our closed off groups about how "for love" we are. I'm guilty of this myself.

But we don't yield much substantive change in doing this. And as much as voting may be a way to act on that alignment with love, and a truly important way to be sure, manifesting love with a group of others who are also for love is what is going to grab the attention and rewrite the hateful rhetoric of the world.

It's high time those pro-love form a murmuration. Take the ordinary and commonplace reality of who we are and attach it to a collective that is beautiful and swirling and mesmerizing and stops everyone in their tracks. Just like the way of the Starling.

The more divisive the world gets, and it seems pretty divisive with this Trump administration, the more the world could benefit from a movement of love as beautiful as a murmuration.

A movement of smiling and acknowledging others' existence. A movement of charity that attaches itself to the faces of other people, not just checkbooks. A movement that works to always, always, always place the human before the ideology. Because every human has love entrenched in them. Unfortunately though, it's often ideology, or specific categories of thought, that taint our ability to see that love.

About Time

The problem with knowing that you are going to marry someone some two years before they are ready for you to ask them to do such a thing is how you have to keep the most exciting realization you've ever had completely to yourself...

Emily and I had been dating for about a year, and things were going well. We had grown as individuals and as a couple, and that was tangible not just in the comfort we felt around each other, but in the friendship and trust we had built.

Although I had had a couple of, as I would say, *mystical* experiences, revelations, spurts of profound emotion, or whatever you want to call them, that led me to truly believe Emily would one day be my wife, there's also the necessity of knowing such an important decision in a tangible way. Not to mention the not-so-tiny tiny detail of Emily needing to grow to feel the same way toward me.

238

The good news is, Emily had started to feel a similar way. And on top of that, the needed tangibility was found through crying together both out of joy and sorrow and encountering every emotion we could imagine between those two extremes. And upon going through the whole course of that spectrum, we still found the other to be the person we desired to turn to time and time again. Which tends to be a fairly good clue that you're experiencing something special.

This experience was no *two ponds with a canal to connect between* philosophy on relationships. This was love. And any metaphor or lesson that speaks to love always falls short of capturing the reality felt.

No longer was the frame of thought "I need Emily," like it had been sophomore year. It was now "I never knew I needed Emily, but now that I know her truly, all the idiosyncrasies of her, from the way she squints to the depth or her past, I can't help but keep going forward alongside her."

And it could be said that coming to that point, through hard work and a reality tied to pulse rather than romanticized idealization, is much more beautiful than having a mystical experience. And definitely a lot more tangible.

Over Christmas break, at the tail end of 2016, I met with a family friend, who is also a jeweler, to talk diamonds. And my mind began to spin with the complexity and price of such a thing. I just wanted to be in love for the rest of my life!

But I did it. I purchased the bribery device of rose gold and sparkle. And had it shipped to Spokane.

The ring was being shipped to Whitworth, and I remember sitting in the coffee shop hitting the refresh button on my email over and over again, knowing that I should be getting a campus post office alert signaling its arrival. The FedEx tracking said it had arrived. I couldn't take it anymore and walked up to the counter and said I had a package that should've been there.

They told me to hold tight to let them sort through everything first.

I told them it was a ring.

They handed me a package.

I took it up to my office on campus and opened the package. I held the symbol of union in my hand. Part of me wanted to drive over and propose on the spot! Love is a bit irrational. But I took a breath. And went back to equilibrium.

I proposed on the shores of Lake Coeur d'Alene, where I had asked Emily to date me to begin with, just over a year ago. And it was this same lake that I had seen on Google Earth as a fifth grader, which led me to want to make a move out to the Pacific Northwest to begin with.

It was a culmination of so many things. And as I stood there, freezing in the winter weather, frozen tears slipping down both of our faces, I was able to read her the letter I had written after watching *About Time* with her two years previous. The letter that was my future-telling proclamation. The letter written *before* Emily turned me down our sophomore year. The one that mentioned how I couldn't wait to read her this note on a very special day. The day we both found ourselves living in that moment.

For someone who found predestination a horribly flawed theological system, I certainly was a fan of it in relation to marriage proposals.

She said yes, and that night we celebrated with all of our friends. And the interesting thing is nothing really changed. We just kept on being in love. Now there was just a heightened commitment attached to it. But it was a steady flow of the same thing. Care and compassion and adoration for another human being.

And I think that that's how love is supposed to be. A road that just keeps going. And we have multiple roads in our lives. Some major. Some minor. Roads of all the people we care about and love.

And perhaps the map of all these roads is also a map of the arteries of God. Each one tied to the pulse of something intimate but greater.

What became clear in that day, though, was that I had just created a road with another person that would be the longest one I had to date. I had a partner to walk down the road with. I wouldn't have to set out into the unknown alone anymore. And as we drove back from Coeur d'Alene that night, I couldn't wait to see all the roads we'd drive down together going forward.

Death as Theme

Israel Nebeker and I were sitting in the glorified closet that is the sound booth of Whitworth's radio station. We were discussing the nature of Israel's latest album with his band, Blind Pilot. The album is titled *And Then, Like Lions*, and it dealt with a series of major shifts in Israel's personal life. Such shifts were also paired with large amounts of pain and grief. The end of a romantic relationship that had lasted thirteen years, a falling out with friends, and the sudden cancer diagnosis of Israel's father all happened within the span of a month.

Such tragedy continued with the eventual passing of his father and, in turn, birthed the opus of *And Then, Like Lions*.

About five months earlier I had sat in another enclosed space. This space was an office in the Whitworth Chapel. The office had no windows except for the hundreds of books littered on shelves, which each seemed to peer into their own worlds. None of which were being discussed now.

In my role as the spiritual life coordinator, I was tasked with meeting with students who felt they had a need they wanted to address on campus that coalesced around the spiritual dynamic at Whitworth. In these meetings, students and I would brainstorm ideas as to how we could act on those needs through some type of programming. The conversation being held in this windowless office in the chapel focused on student mental health. The seasons were shifting into darker and drearier months, but there were more reasons than just the shorter days for this discussion.

One of the students in the room, of which there were three, including myself, as well as one professor, brought up news I was unaware of. Apparently, since the beginning of that academic year, there had been a surprising amount of parent deaths amongst the student body. The professor brought facts to the sadness by saying there had been at least five such passing's only two months into the year.

My mind immediately went to the album I had been listening to for much of the second half of the summer, Blind Pilot's *And Then, Like Lions*. On it, there were songs focusing on the exact same thing. Songs Israel wrote as he wrestled with he pain and difficulty of his fathers passing. I brought up the idea of reaching out to Israel, inviting him to come to campus, play music from the album, and discuss how he used art as a means of working through loss. The rest of the group enjoyed the idea. A Facebook message was sent twenty minutes later, and a response came five minutes after that.

And that's why, that March, Israel and I found ourselves

sitting in the sound booth talking about the nature of loss.

. . .

I, fortunate as I have been, had not encountered loss firsthand in my life. As the twenty-two-year-old I was at the time, all of my grandparents were still alive. Death was a concept for me. A concept that, because of the distance between it and I, I had been able to develop theory around through philosophical inquiry, rather than reality. A Mike Christie pastime.

But it's one thing to entertain an idea, and it's another to live within its grasp. And it was through loving Emily that the grasp of such a thing became real.

Emily's mother suffered from bipolar disorder for most of Emily's life growing up. There were strings of euphoric mania and strings of crippling depression. There were times of heightened spending of any money she had accumulated, only to be struck back into a times of poverty. These highs and lows were by-products of the treacherous disease that Emily, as a child, watched take hold of her mother.

Bipolar disorder is death and resurrection of the worst kind.

Over and over, lulls and vitality. Both on such extreme ends of the spectrum that they were impossible to keep pace with. When Emily was a junior in high school, her mom lost the battle of the horrid and too-scarcely-talked about reality of mental illness.

She took her own life.

The weight of something like this can't be supported by the pages of a book. It can't be supported by countless condolence cards. And it certainly can't be supported by the theories spouted off by, at the time when such theories were spouted, a fiancé who held all sorts of ideas concerning how, why, and what death is.

Only experiencing death firsthand or talking to someone who has tasted the reality of death, sitting with them in their pain but not trying to offer solutions, listening, and speaking only as they are ready, can pave the way for authentic knowledge of what death is.

And even then, if you haven't experienced it yourself, it's likely you'll still fall short. And as much as I wanted to bring Israel to campus for those students who had lost parents that year, I mostly wanted to bring him to campus for the girl I loved. To be able to create a conversation about death that was accessible and available.

. . .

"I found myself needing to get out in nature a lot in the years following my Dad's death," Israel said.

He continued in a mild-mannered tone,

"I was living along this beautiful stretch of the Oregon coast at the time. There were these trees I'd run through, and they opened up to the Pacific. One particular morning, I made my way through this clearing of trees. The moon was sitting right above the surface of the ocean. It looked just like a painting my Dad would've painted (Israel's father,

Royal Nebeker, is a world renowned painter). And in that moment and in that place, in some unexplainable way, I knew he was still there. And that's where the song "Moon at Dawn" comes from."

The whole album *And Then, Like Lions*, which is where the song detailing this encounter appears on, was framed by this phrase Israel coined:

"The past isn't finished with us yet."

This line shows how Israel viewed memory and meaning after the initial processing of a time littered with deep difficulty and grief.

We chatted about the nature of death. He told me how he began to see his father in new ways after he passed. In ways more than just the scope of the title of *father*. He began to see him through the eyes of others.

And through doing so, he saw him as a mentor to art students. As a husband to his mother. As a friend to community members. It opened up the perception he had for his dad.

Around the time of this event and this specific conversation, I had become strategic in the way in which I talked about theology. A lot of my critiques and frustrations about how Christianity had been historically framed had gained language. And the mantra I would tell anyone, even if they didn't ask for a deep conversation about theology, was that spirituality is much more of a theme than it is a category. Something I believed many in the religious world had flip-flopped.

My assertion was that people have an unhelpful tendency. And this tendency is viewing God as a category, or object, or tangible existence when God, to my understanding, is much more of a theme.

A river, as opposed to a pond.

What Israel seemed to be saying about his Dad was similar but about those that have passed on.

"Do you think what happened with your perception of your father after his death was you began to see who he was more as a theme alive in the world rather than a category existing in the world," I asked.

Israel nodded and smiled.

"Yeah, I think that's extremely astute. Especially for someone who hasn't experienced loss. I think I began to see him more by the qualities that existed within him, rather than the walking talking person he was. And the beautiful thing about seeing someone like that is that even when they are *gone* they can never actually be gone," he said.

What I've come to understand, even if death hasn't made residence in my neighborhood, is that people are not just bags of flesh. And that even when the flesh is lost, the person is not. Because it was when Jesus died that the spirit came. And is it not spirit that allows us to encounter God on a daily basis?

Spirit is breath and wind and moving air.

Spirit is the thing all around us, embracing us with a presence much more than just the physical category of something.

When we see the theme of something, we see it existing eternally. Playfully at times, shyly at others, and we begin to realize it's all around us.

In the morning moon.

In the mysterious way of water.

In the bread and the wine of a dinner party.

What once was always will be. All it asks is our willing participation to *see* it / she / him / they in ways beyond simply sight.

Israel himself does not fall within or label himself with a specific belief system. And yet the theme his art speaks to is one focused on giving new life to things that may be gone in the ways in which they once were alive. Giving language to the places where he has encountered and feels the presence of such people and things.

This theme or idea tied to his music, quite frankly, holds a much more vibrant pulse to the reality of death and resurrection than a lot of the stale sermons I've heard on Easter Sunday. Because this way of perceiving people post loss keeps them very much alive – in new and exciting ways. All around us.

. . .

Israel delivered an unbelievably beautiful performance at Whitworth. We had him play in the chapel; alone with his guitar, and he and I did a Q&A in the middle of the set. It was really quite magical. And given his band Blind Pilot are one of my all-time favorites, I was a bit star-struck.

He would preface every song with a story, and one of the most memorable stories was the one tied to the song "Don't Doubt." He reminisced about how, as he was writing music for the new album, a high schooler across the street from where he was living was going through a really difficult time. And Israel, knowing the family, wanted to find a way to instill some hope into the kid. To share the message of always choosing life. But he also was struggling to figure out how to do that without appealing to something spiritual that the two of them might not have shared.

But hope has a way of making itself known in weird places, and Israel went on to say that the place hope revealed itself to him was his mother's arugula garden. Where, as he sat amidst a heaping patch of the stuff, he realized that the way of the arugula was exactly the hope he was looking for for the song. Because it was a reminder that life always keeps going. That it keeps coming back.

Because just a few months ago, his moms garden was simply dirt, but now, with spring, arugula was littered about. And to choose to go with life because of that. Because life is always the resilient one that finds its way back to the surface of reality. This idea is highlighted by the following line from the song:

"Don't doubt. Even your breath is breathing for another one. Don't you just take the dark way out."

After Israel left, I was struck by how beautiful his performance was, but was also struck with this tale. Because what it spoke to is the choice we all have in regard to what we will do with / how we will handle difficulties in our life. This arugula story spoke to the same reality of people existing beyond their physical categories. It spoke to the notion that he had framed the whole album in, "the past isn't finished with us yet."

And as much as Israel was a wonderful spokesperson for those thoughts, I also felt compelled, as did the small group coordinators I worked with, to follow the event up with something students could participate in rather than just sit and witness like they did with a concert.

And that's where abandoned dorms come in handy.

A Haunted House for Your Soul

"Once upon a midnight dreary, while I pondered weak and weary..." - Edgar Allen Poe

We don't, as human beings, practice the art of being introspective very often. Because if we did, the quote above from Edgar Allen Poe wouldn't be seen as spooky so much as it would be seen as natural. There is something that happens when you have to enter inside your own mind and thought.

A historical mystic named Teresa of Ávila was big on this. She had an experience titled *The Dark Night of the Soul*, an experience she believed necessary in order for humans to truly become in tune with God in their life.

If death is a theme, then so too is life. And to become conscious of a theme, we have to become conscious of the influences that we have hitting us at any one time. But because we are so easily distracted, recognizing those influences becomes nearly impossible.

That is, unless, in the stillness of the midnight dark, feeling altogether weak and weary, we ponder. And introspect.

. . .

Back in 1974, Spokane, Washington, hosted the World's Fair. Don't ask me why or how, but they did. Whenever you host the World's Fair, you typically have people from around the world in your town. And whenever you have an event that draws a global audience, you usually have a lot of people. And whenever you have a lot of people, you need a lot of housing. And that is why, at least to my knowledge, there are three old seventies-inspired residence halls on Whitworth's campus, known, perhaps ironically given the worldly inspiration that led to their construction, as The Village. The Village was used as extra housing for the World Fair all those years ago. And it's seen better days. A bit weathered and a bit dated, it is no real surprise that during my senior year at Whitworth, one of its buildings, known as Akili, was abandoned entirely.

Throughout my senior year, I had become close with the Resident Director of The Village, Brian, and his wife, Andra. Both were in the whole mystical-spiritual-but-not-religious realm that I had been categorizing myself in. Andra and I hung out at least once a week with all the other small group coordinators that year, as she was helping Mindy out with logistics in the realm of campus ministry. Brian and I had talked a few different times over lunch about doing a campus event together. And, in early spring, right before all the flowers began to bud again, we decided to take advantage of the vacant building he oversaw. And we did this by filtering our whole purpose through the lens of a parable by an author we both held respect for—Peter Rollins. That name again.

Rollins believes we are all haunted houses. We are full of ghosts. Ghosts of those we've lost, ghosts of past pains or difficulties, ghosts of all we've been through. In each of us, Rollins says, there are poltergeists and holy ghosts.

Poltergeists are the type of ghost we pretend isn't there, those past troubles that we repress. But poltergeists, by their very definition, come out and haunt us in the most unlikely and unfortunate of times.

And then there are the holy ghosts. The ghosts that we confront and turn into something new. They are the new life to the death that once consumed us.

To give people a chance to recognize, as Israel said at his event, "the past isn't finished with us yet" we had an idea to construct something I coined a *haunted house for the soul*. A place where students would have an interactive experience that would offer them the opportunity to open up to things that they had repressed.

. . .

I once read somewhere that the musician Sufjan Stevens is where the hipster and Jesus intersect. Although I am not a person falling into said hipster category, I had found that Stevens did make me think of Jesus. And loud, complicated noises – but that's beside the point.

It was Stevens that offered a painfully wonderful framework that partnered in tandem with Rollins' parable and Israel's perspective for the event.

Stevens lost his mother in 2013. She had been estranged most of his life. She struggled with mental illness and was detached for much of Stevens' upbringing in Michigan. In hopes of processing through the grief of his mother's passing, Stevens released what is, in my and the music blog Pitchfork's opinion, one of the greatest folk albums of the past decade. It's titled *Carrie & Lowell* and its opening song, "Death with Dignity," tied Israel, Teresa of Ávila, Rollins, Poe, and this event together perfectly.

"Spirit of my silence, I can hear you. And I long to be near you. But I don't know where to begin. I don't know where to begin."

If you are trying to open people up to an experience in which they can confront the troubles that they have carried around but don't want to address, this line, delivered so delicately by Stevens, is the perfect thing to play as you shut them into a dark hallway for five minutes.

. . .

The night before the event, a bunch of student leaders helped me drape the hallway on the first floor with a black tarp. This was the first of four phases of the event. And it was by far the most dreary. We coined it *The Ghost Hallway*, and it was made as dark as possible. The only lighting came from Christmas lights that were hung over a series of signs outlining the Rollins parable about us being haunted houses. Students made their way around the hallway a couple of times as the song "Death with Dignity" played in the background. It was definitely a bit of an eerie environment. And its intent was to mirror the parts of our memory or soul that we know exists, but we prefer to leave unnoticed.

You may be thinking this sounds remarkably insensitive given what some students likely had gone through. Don't worry, so do I. But my team and I met with the counseling department on campus to make sure what we posted and shared were okay and avoided triggers. There was also a licensed counselor on call if someone were to have uncovered something heavy and needed some professional guidance.

The signs, in order, outlined the Rollins parable in abbreviated form.

Sign one: We are all haunted houses. We are all full of ghosts.

Sign two: Ghosts holding the memories of those we've lost. That which has pained us. Our troubled stories.

Sign three: There are two types of these ghosts inside us.

Sign four: There are the poltergeists. The ghosts we repress and avoid. Only to be haunted by in the most unlikely and unfortunate of times.

Sign five: And then there are the holy ghosts.

Sign six: The ghosts we gain when we expose and address our darkness. And transform it into

. . .

Renewal.

Sign seven: It is what we do with our stories that determines the ghosts we carry.

Sign eight: Which ghosts will you allow to reside within?

As students entered the room, they were greeted by those lines from Stevens' "Death with Dignity" ringing out of a hidden speaker,

"Spirit of my silence I can hear you, but I'm scared to be near you, because I don't know where to begin."

After the duration of the song, students were led to the next room. They were greeted by the low lighting of lamps. Andra was seated in a chair that students gathered around. She, having a masters degree in spiritual direction, led a guided meditation which encouraged students to be open to letting whatever ghosts were within them to be recognized. To let the pains of the past not be hidden by repression but be opened up and brought to light.

From here students went upstairs to a room with a giant canvas tarp. At the top of the stairs, the light illuminated the rooms in a much fuller way than the rooms down below. Around the canvas tarp, there were materials for writing or drawing to give students the chance of exposing a ghost they may have artistically.

The last stage was a mirrored hallway to the one below. But this one was illuminated with an assortment of warm lighting, had walls lined with Bible verses of renewal and Mary Oliver quotes, and had the hallways lined with hundreds upon hundreds of flowers donated by Trader Joe's. The door to the emergency exit students were to exit from had a sign reminding them that the death and renewal like what they had just experienced is all around them and is inviting them to participate in acts of restoration. And that by leaving from the second floor, they were leaving on a different trajectory. A trajectory which invited them to transcend what they had walked in with, while also including it in their story.

. . .

Often times we are quick to want to move past the hard and the difficult. I'm totally guilty of this. But the ghosts, the things dwelling in the spirit of our silence, are actually banging at the door of our reality begging to be let out. I'm convinced of this.

And like Rollin's said, they are going to come out, we just get to dictate how and in what forms. Israel's event helped me realize that the past doesn't have to be finished with us. And this event, through looking at what was written and drawn on that canvas tarp, in the third stage where people were given the chance to express, clued me in on just how much potential the negative has when given a second chance.

Final words don't have to be final words. The things we don't want to access can actually launch into new and beautiful things. It may take time. But I think it's there. It's a reality encountered on albums by bands, in compost piles, and the seasons and life cycles around us. The past isn't finished. The story always has another chapter.

Graduate

As time at Whitworth wore down, things began to feel more and more unsettled. You don't realize how rooted you are in something until you have to uproot. And anyone who has spent anytime removing big plants knows that taking something planted in the dirt, out, is far harder than putting something out of the dirt, in. My senior year had been a time of personal development. Profound growth and confidence in the identity I had worked to shape. I had community in truly beautiful ways. I felt known at Whitworth. I could walk around and say hello to an assortment of people. I had been given an outlet to turn ideas into reality through my job. Perhaps more than anything, though, I had mentors.

Mindy, in particular, had become a friend of incredible closeness. I was in her office almost daily. We would talk about anything and everything. She was a boss, a professor I had been a TA for, and a close friend. Emily and I had become close to the rest of her family—her husband Kyle, and daughters, Syd and Ash. And I could go into her office and just spew out thoughts and feelings and emotions. It was really difficult knowing that upon graduation, the causal stop-ins to her office weren't going to be routine anymore.

And then there was the knowledge of a parting from Spokane in a broader sense. Leaving places like Branches and the wisdom and inspiration from people like Ryan. Ryan and I, as I've already stated, tracked. He felt like someone who I could go to whenever I lost my sense of direction because of how clearly in-line our ideas were. He was a person I could rant to about frustrations with Christianity, and bring up any aspect of that without the fear of being judged.

There was the pain of leaving the housemate dynamic I had with Luke, Joseph, John, Dalton, and Chris. Even if I didn't spend an overabundance of time there between school, spending time with Em, and my job, there would be no more outrageous antics with them anymore. No more pranks, like the time we took a metal chain, strung it through all of John's clothes, locked it shut, and sent him on a scavenger hunt to find the key. No more tennis ball golf, where we'd throw tennis balls over the house toward a metal bucket, and whoever made it in with the least throws won. No more Wii golf with a controller in one hand and a beer in the other. No more house shows of drunken philosophical ranting with one of our favorite singer-songwriters. Bryan had come back that spring to play a show in our backyard and the same type of antics that happened in the fall of the Whitworth event happened that time too.

Emily and I had decided to move to Tacoma when we graduated. I had a summer internship that supposedly had the potential to become a full-time job, and Emily had had her nursing practicum at a Tacoma hospital. Our wedding was slotted to occur in that area on September 3. There were a whole bunch of incredible new beginnings on the horizon, but a whole bunch of good past and presents slipping away. It was a weird time for the mind to process. Which is what has to happen with any transition.

I still didn't know what I wanted to do with my life. I was set to work at a nonprofit for an internship set up by the Whitworth Office of Church Engagement. But, as I'll point to in a minute, that wasn't at all a promising plan for the future. All and all, I wasn't ready to leave the comfort of what was. Which, as life often points to, can turn out to be the most necessary time to leave. Because when you are fond of something, it still exists within the realm of appreciation. Which is a far better place to leave it than in a state of resentment or detachment.

Life had been order, disorder, and then reorder. And I didn't want to leave it. But certain spectrums of reorder can become order after too long of a time of comfort and complacency. So, it was time for some disorder again.

As the summer wore on, Emily and I had a harder and harder time finding work that would set us up for success after our wedding. The situation got a bit desperate. The internship that I had been doing with a fellow Whitworth

Grad named Josiah turned into a disaster. There was no work to be had in it and our boss was a complete space cadet. Josiah uses a wheel chair, something our boss knew going into the summer because Whitworth had him promise the workplace and the homestay would be accessible.

Neither were. And our boss seemed to be completely blind as to how that would be a problem. Being so clueless as to ask Josiah why he always had to use the door further away from the parking lot. To which Josiah would pointedly reply, "because the one you like using has steps. And I use a wheelchair."

Josiah and I also were given no projects because there was no work to be had. This non-profit was on its last leg, and it became clear to us that there would be no work to be had with them after the summer internship was over.

Graduation didn't seem to be leading to any liberation like it was supposed to; it was more binding. All hopes of a big future had turned into worry. And whenever a once hope turns into a worry, it can leave you struggling to find anything to cling to. Emily and I learned how to cling to each other during this time, even when each of us was at such a low point in our esteem. There were days where we didn't offer the other much to grab onto.

We began to think outside the realm of Tacoma for our future, which ended up being the solution. Because with less than two weeks until our wedding day, as we were driving to premarital counseling, where the first question would be, "What are your plans with not having jobs?"

Emily's phone rang.

"Hello?"

"Hello, is this Emily Fisher?"

"Yes, it is."

"Hi, Emily, this is Trish from Sacred Heart Medical Center in Spokane. I just wanted to call and let you know that after reviewing your application we'd like to offer you a job with us! It starts September 18."

I heard all this over the speaker. September 18th was six days after we got back from our honeymoon. Just enough time to pack up and move over. We both started tearing up.

The week and a half before our wedding was a mad scramble, as it is for most. But on top of the decorating and food logistics and family flying into town, we got to search around online for a place to live, sign a lease on an apartment, and begin to get our things into boxes to move back to where everything had started.

Spokane.

Conclusion — Antimatter

One of the more head-banging bands that I was into during high school was called Manchester Orchestra. Their song "Shake it Out" was on regular rotation in my earbuds as I laced up my skates in the locker rooms of John Lindell Ice Arena. The obsession with this band eventually filtered its way down to the next up-and-coming male Christie, my brother Colin.

And the summer those two affinities for one band intersected was this summer of post-graduation and marriage.

And it was on their latest album that I was in to a little invisible secret floating all around.

Colin had been texting me over and over about how I had to listen to Manchester Orchestra's 2017 album, A Black Mile to the Surface. I hadn't listened to them since my hockey days and looked back on them with a little bit of cynicism because their music was tied to my high school years. But Colin pestered, I obliged, and Josiah and I listened to it in the car going to and from work all summer. We would blare it from the speakers to distract us from the consistently frustrating work situation we found ourselves in.

Unlike what I had previously associated Manchester Orchestra with, songs on this album didn't make me feel like I should be lacing up hockey skates. Instead, they led me to want to sit down and enter into the story Andy Hull, lead singer and lyricist, was painting. And in order to grasp a story, you have to have an idea of the setting.

And that's where things got interesting.

The album was centered around a tiny town called Lead, South Dakota. Colin and I battled endlessly about its pronunciation. The verdict is still out. Lead used to be a booming mining village located in the Black Hills. The same hills where presidents' faces found a canvas on Mount Rushmore. Because of the gold rush that places like the Black Hills experienced, Lead is home to Homestake Mine.

Homestake Mine was the most productive gold mine in the Western Hemisphere and remains the deepest at 8,240 feet.

Deep, to say the least.

But gold mining slowed steadily, and the mine shut down. So what do you do when you close down a mine with a one-and-a-half-mile-deep hole? You can't just fill the hole back in with the dirt you dug out of it. So, you do the only thing you can do—

You use it study the secrets of our universe.

Homestake Mine is now a laboratory that studies dark matter and antimatter. And antimatter caught my imagination the most. And all these thoughts and revelations came because some random band two Christie boys both loved in high school made an album.

And the more we listened to this album, and the more we learned about antimatter, the more meaning we drew out of both.

. . .

The substance of the universe is referred to as matter, and matter is composed of billions of things called atoms. You probably learned that in middle school. Atoms, like humans, have traits that make them what they are. The most basic and elementary of these traits are an atom's protons, neutrons, and electrons.

Likely none of this is new to you. Most of us can remember such things from school. Protons have their positive charge. Neutrons neutral. Electrons negative.

The thing you likely didn't learn in eighth-grade science, though, was that there is something called antimatter that exists in the universe as well. When the universe began, many scientists believe that there were nearly equal parts matter and antimatter, and can't quite figure out why there's so much more matter nowadays.

When matter and its anti-brother interact, they annihilate

and release energy. Back in 2015, scientists were able to view antimatter for around fifteen minutes in a vacuum located in a research lab in Switzerland. What they found was what they expected. In the antihydrogen they observed, there were protons, neutrons, and electrons.

But the protons were negative, neutrons still neutral, and electrons positive.

Antimatter was matter flipped. It was 100 percent the same thing, but 100 percent different.

Even though its characteristics were reversed from its matter counterpart making it theoretically something 100 percent different, a theoretical universe comprised of antimatter rather than matter is thought to look exactly like the one we live in now. It would be 100 percent the same.

So, what that means is that there are two realities in the universe that we live in that are 100 percent the same, yet, at the same time, 100 percent different.

Colin and I were in constant conversation as I learned about all of this, and our minds were spinning. We picked up on references throughout the album that seemed to speak to this.

But then antimatter began to have a bigger impact. One of personal significance.

I was in the midst of the biggest transitional phase of my life. I had graduated from college and was going to be getting married in about a month. One of the most consistent worries I have is not staying true to who I am as an individual. And while in this season of transition, I was thinking about this a lot. Antimatter helped me realize that even if my life was about to be 100 percent different, I could still remain 100 percent me.

The reality of antimatter gave truth to the idea that paradox and truth are perfect partners and gave affirmation to the idea that new circumstances don't necessarily disrupt or corrupt you; you can shift and still be true to yourself.

You can still be 100 percent you but grow to be 100 percent new in how you see, be, and interact with the world. Shifts don't compromise that, they expand it. Whether it is marriage, graduation, or whatever it may be. Newness expands.

And the "still you, but new" idea... that's the goal of all spirituality. That's baptism. That's what it looks like to have the courage to move from order to disorder to reorder. That's seeing a firefly, but then seeing a totally different firefly. And realizing that although it's a different firefly, it's the same light. And the light is what matters. Not catching one form of it.

We all live in this paradox. And because of it, progress should never be feared. Because it is this same/different reality that the universe has been operating under since the beginning of time. It's okay to move. It's necessary. The moment you see something new is the moment you know you're uncovering a secret speaking to the truth of life. A truth that is all around us.

You can pursue something new and still be you. Something different or seen as heretical or *for* something you've been taught to be *against*.

Even if people are scared that you're doing so. Even if people say you are on a slippery slope. Even if the people around you don't understand.

It's okay to pursue your hallelujah for the first time.

To enter the river and leave the pond.

All of that is good and beautiful and necessary.

Because all of that is a sign that you are moving. You are reordering. You are becoming you. And that's beautiful. That's renewal. That's recognizing the Insistence of something Divine. That's bringing heaven here, as opposed to there. That's learning to see.

And that's freeing.

Special Thanks

Thank you first and foremost to YOU for taking time out your life to make it all the way to the end notes. That's impressive.

Thank you to Emily for your patience as I spouted off ideas and spent too much money on coffee and cinnamon scones while writing this. You're the best steen there is.

Thank you to my parents who put up with laggy phone call connection and let me read this to them over and over and over and... you get it. You guys gave me such a wonderful life growing up and embodied an image of love winning. Which has made it that much more accessible for me to understand.

Thank you to my editor, Carrie Olschner. Carrie, you know first hand the struggle I have with grammar and cohesive thought. You are a saint. Without you this would have been a jumbled mush of words.

Kevin, thank you for accompanying me to Rockwood time and time again and adhering to a friendship of silence as I typed, typed, and typed some more. For not being mentioned in this book, you were a pivotal source of encouragement. Maybe the next one? Ha!

Patrick, thank you for writing a forward and for being a friend who, although is far away, always yields profound insight and an abundance of encouragement regarding all things spiritual.

Mentors like Mindy, Dayna, Kent, Ryan, and many others, thank you for encouraging me to use my voice. And for showing me that ideas matter, and therefore should become physical matter.

And then there is this...

This book was a dream at first. But dreams are, by their nature, not physical. Physicality requires resources. Being young, newly married, and in a fair amount of student debt, I didn't have those resources readily available, so I turned to kickstarter. And family and friends came up huge. To all of you listed below... wow. Thank you, thank you, THANK YOU a million times over.

Jenny and Justin Warns
Whitney Jester
Mara Kramer
Susan Rusinowski
Reagan Kissel
Sarah and Daniel Small

Kylie Guenther

Courtney and Nick Shea

The Stone Family

Mom and Dad Christie

Suzie and Mark Merruci

Kathy and Jordan Tenjeras

Tim Skoczek

Andra and Bryan Dennis

Doug and Marg Forier

Shelley and Dennis Fiore

Craig Ward

Jeff Lanctot

Carole and Denny Mascioli

Anita Heap

Aunt Linda and Uncle Bob

Mike and Dianne Lueck

Dayna and Jim Jones

Chris MacMurray

Chris Zangkas

Aunt MB and Uncle Terry

Teagan and Amelia Brown

Noah Lovins

Kevin Glover

The Mackey Family

Mike Pero

Jill and Richard Kirsammer

Phil Gathany

Jack Christie

Liz Visci

Bre Lyons
Robin Miller
Nonnie and Papa
Christie and Scott Simony
Josiah Vanwingerden
Sandy Karolak
The Crimmins Family
John Marshall

Books and authors and other works that have influenced this book

Rob Bell
What is the Bible
Love Wins
What We Talk About When We Talk About God
The Robcast
The Zimzum of Love

Peter Rollins
The Orthodox Heretic and Other Impossible Tales
The Divine Magician

John Caputo
What Would Jesus Deconstruct

Emergence

Mary Oliver
Upstream
Felicity

Wendell Berry
The Country of Marriage

Bohumil Hrabal
Too Loud a Solitude

Netflix - Chefs Table
Alinea and Greg Achatz

Death Cab for Cutie
Kintsugi

The Mowgli's
Waiting for the Dawn

Bryan John Appleby
Fire on the Vine
The Narrow Valley

Manchester Orchestra
A Black Mile to the Surface

Sufjan Stevens
Carrie and Lowell

Night Beds
Ivywild
Country Sleep

Blind Pilot
And Then, Like Lions

The Head and the Heart
Rivers and Roads

On Being Podcast with Krista Tippett
Richard Rohr episode

Richard Rohr
Daily Meditations can be found at CAC.org
Falling Upward

Mitch Albom
Tuesdays with Morie

About the Author

Mike Christie lives in Spokane with his wife, Emily and his dog, Oliver. When Oliver isn't biting his hand, you can likely find Mike either eating scones at Rockwood Bakery with his friend Kevin, wandering around the parks of Spokane's South Hill with Emily, or playing shuffle board at Steel Barrel tap room. Mike works at Branches church where he coordinates services and speaks from time to time. If you want to get ahold of Mike, you can via his blog located at mikechristie.net. He'd love to get to know you / hear about your ideas and what inspires you and all that jazz.

Made in the USA
Monee, IL
06 July 2020